Known by
Your Fruit

Known by Your Fruit

(Formerly *Walking in the Fruit of the Spirit*)

By Sharon Daugherty

Known by Your Fruit
ISBN 978-1-56267-625-4
(Former Title: *Walking in the Fruit of the Spirit* ISBN 1-56267-181-2)
Copyright © 1984, 1998, 2007 by Sharon Daugherty
Victory Christian Center
7700 South Lewis Avenue
Tulsa, OK 74136

CONTENTS

Preface

Introduction

Conclusion

PREFACE

You will know them by their fruits. Do men gather grapes from thornbushes or figs from thistles?

Matthew 7:16 NKJV

Jesus said that every tree is known or identified by the fruit it bears. You either demonstrate good fruit or bad fruit. Whatever is inside of you will come out of you. When you squeeze a lemon, sour juice comes out. The squeeze didn't make the juice sour. It was already sour. The squeeze simply allowed what was inside of the lemon to come out.

We're living in times that Paul wrote about in Second Timothy 3:1 AMP – "times of great stress and trouble [hard to deal with and hard to bear]." This creates a pressure or a squeeze in people's lives, and whatever is on the inside of them begins to be revealed. Some people hide behind a mask as long as there is no pressure. However, in times like these, many masks will come off.

Being genuine and making efforts to live your life submitted to Jesus must be a priority to each of us as Christians. If we live like the world around us, then when difficulties, tests, and trials come, we could fall apart. Right now, many who are going through tests and trials are falling apart. Who will they look to for help if Christians also fall apart? Jesus needs us to be stable and secure in what we believe and in the One for whom we stand.

Can people see stability in our lives? Can people see Jesus in the way we live? Or do they see a mixture of the world and Him? Jesus' words are still speaking to us today: **"If any man will come after me, let him** (her) **deny himself** (herself)**, and take up his** (her) **cross daily, and follow me"** (Luke 9:23).

Standing steadfast and immoveable in our relationship with Jesus and His call upon our lives will require humility, faith, surrender, self-denial and love that go beyond our human

vii

reasonings. Self-denial runs opposite to the direction the world thinks. However, Jesus denied Himself in order to love the world He was called to save. Some people don't like to hear words about self-denial. They like to do whatever they want to do and believe God's grace gives them freedom to live like the world around them. However, Jesus calls us to live differently – by the standard of His Word and the leading of His Holy Spirit.

In this book you'll come to understand the fruit of the Spirit and how you can grow in His fruit. God wants people everywhere to know and experience who He is through your life. You've been placed in the earth by God to be His witness. Jesus says <u>they will know you by your fruit</u>.

INTRODUCTION

Have you ever seen someone you admired at a distance and thought they were so great that they could surely not have human flaws or weaknesses like other people? Let me encourage you. Every Christian has had flaws and weaknesses that they have had to bring into surrender and submission to the lordship of Jesus Christ. The only perfect Man who has lived on earth is Jesus Christ, the Son of God.

The good news is that when a person receives Jesus into his or her heart, He comes in with His overcoming power and His grace to help us rise above the flaws and weaknesses. He gives us His supernatural strength to subdue and conquer the flesh. Knowing that we can't subdue and conquer the sin nature in our own ability keeps us in a position of humility and dependence upon God. This does not mean we have to accept sin and human weakness as just a part of our lives here on earth. Instead, it means we can walk free from the control of sin and the fleshly pull of the world around us by yielding to the promptings of the Holy Spirit and renewing our minds to God's Word and obeying what His Word says. Sometimes Christians resign themselves to think that everyone sins in thought, word, or deed daily, so why make the effort to overcome any flaw or weakness?

In Mark 11:12-26, Jesus and the disciples were walking and Jesus was hungry. He saw a fig tree at a distance, thinking He would eat some of the fruit from it. When He came to the tree and looked closer, although it had leaves, it had no fruit. *Dake's* Bible shares that "fig trees came in two varieties; the early fig tree and the late fig tree. Figs appear before or with the leaves, so the leaves indicated that the tree must have figs, even though the time of figs to be fully ripe was not yet come."[1] This is why Jesus expected there to be fruit on the tree. He spoke to the tree and said, "No man eat fruit of you hereafter for ever"(v.14). The disciples heard Him speak to the tree and didn't say anything at that moment.

The next day as they passed by the tree again, it was dried up from the roots. Peter said, "Master, the fig tree You cursed is withered away." Jesus then began to teach the disciples about the power of words that we speak when we believe in what we are saying. Interestingly, He follows the teaching on words with a teaching on keeping your heart free from unforgiveness and says, "If you don't forgive other people, God will not forgive you of your sins and shortcomings. However, if you are a forgiving person, God will forgive you when you need forgiveness."

Sometimes Christians think that salvation and going to heaven are just dependent upon their asking Jesus to come into their hearts at some time in their lives. We have to realize that this is only the beginning. Our life in Christ is a <u>walk</u>. We've been called to <u>walk in the</u> Spirit so we won't fulfill the lust of the flesh (Gal. 5:16). That's why Paul wrote in Philippians 2:12,13: **"...work out your own salvation with fear and trembling. For it is God which worketh in you both to <u>will</u> and to <u>do</u> of his good pleasure."** Once you've received salvation through faith in the grace of God, you then have to "work out" or make the effort to walk like Jesus. Some Christians don't want to make any effort, but Jesus said if you're going to come after Him, you'll have to deny yourself (Luke 9:23) and be a doer of His Word. Otherwise, you'll be self-deceived (James 1:22).

Second Peter 1:5-8 NKJV says, **"...giving all diligence, add to your faith virtue, to virtue knowledge, to knowledge self-control, to self-control perseverance, to perseverance godliness, to godliness brotherly kindness, and to brotherly kindness love. For if these things are yours and abound, you will be neither <u>barren</u> nor <u>unfruitful</u> in the knowledge of our Lord Jesus Christ."** Peter encourages us as Christians to give all diligence (<u>make every effort on a continual basis</u>) to add to your faith—virtue (moral excellence), knowledge, self-control, perseverance, godliness, brotherly kindness and agape love (love that's unconditional; a love that forgives and forbears with others; love that does what will benefit others before benefitting oneself; love that's in spite of what others do; love that endures and doesn't stop; a love that is unselfish). When you make the effort to walk in these qualities on a daily basis, you will not become unfruitful or barren spiritually. Verses 9 and 10 go on to say that you won't become spiritually blind (deceived) and fall away from your relationship with God.

Friend, Peter would not have warned us to give diligence to walk in these qualities if there was no possibility of failing to make our calling and election sure. For a person to think that all they need to do is pray a prayer to ask Jesus Christ into their hearts and not pursue to walk after Him but live the rest of their lives fulfilling their lusts is deceptive thinking.

When someone prays sincerely surrendering his/her life to ask Jesus Christ to come into his/her heart and be Lord as well as Savior, they will want to bring their lives into submission to His lordship. There will be an awareness of grieving God if they sin. There is an awesome fire of God and love for God that creates a desire within to honor Him and not be a stumbling block to others. Instead of seeing what they can get away with and compromise in, they have a determination to avoid situations that could create a vulnerability for sin. Genuine Christianity will cause a person to bear fruit that others can see. We realize that any Christian will at some time sin or miss the mark, but a surrendered Christian's heart will be convicted to repent and not continue in the sin.

The twelve disciples of Jesus revealed their human failures and wrong attitudes at times, but they were committed to forsake the things around them to follow Jesus. They wanted to conform to Jesus' way of thinking. They were willing to do whatever He said. After the Day of Pentecost, their passion for Jesus moved them to be willing to give their lives for the One they believed in. Today in our society, people want a little of

Jesus and a little of the world and its lusts. More and more the call of God is drawing Christians to lay down worldly thinking and embrace God's Word in the way they think. Fruit-bearing Christians will stand out and be noticed. Jesus said, **"...by their fruits ye shall know them"** (Matt. 7:20).

The word "fruitful" (in the Greek is *karpophoreo*) means fertile; fruitbearing (very productive). The word "unfruitful" (in the Greek is *akarpos*) means without fruit; not producing good effects upon others; not producing good works; barren (taken from another Greek word *argos* meaning inactive, lazy; useless, idle, unproductive, not producing; empty, devoid, lacking interest, boring, dull). The word "barren" means bringing no useful results.

It's time to do a fruit check in your life. Paul wrote in Second Corinthians 13:5, **"Examine yourselves, whether ye be in the faith** [This is not referring to believing for answered prayer; it refers to your relationship with Jesus and your walk with Him]; **prove your own selves** [test yourself – be honest with yourself]. **Know ye not your own selves, how that Jesus Christ is in you, except ye be reprobates?"** (Greek word *adokimos* meaning rejected; castaway.)

John 15:2 AMP says, **"Any branch in Me that does not bear fruit [that stops bearing] He cuts away (trims off, takes away); and He cleanses and repeatedly prunes every branch that continues to bear fruit, to make it bear more and richer and more excellent fruit."** Sometimes the tests and trials we walk through may seem hard, but if we realize after the test or trimming time that we will bring forth more fruit, then we draw on the grace of God to walk through the test or trial and believe for God's goodness to support and surround us. We then can believe that God will cause things to work together for good in our lives and in our circumstances. (Rom. 8:28.)

It takes diligence to keep our lives in surrender and submission to God's authority, but that is what God requires. Jesus kept Himself in surrender and submission to His Father and He calls us to do the same. This is the place we will find His grace to live fruitful lives. The place of surrender and submission is our position to overcome in this life and to help others overcome.

"Herein is my Father glorified, that ye bear much fruit; so shall ye be my disciples" (John 15:8).

Sharon Daugherty

---

1   Finis Jennings Dake. *Dake's Annotated Reference Bible*, Lawrenceville, GA: Dake Bible Sales, Inc., 1963, 1991, p. 47.

CHAPTER 1
WALKING IN THE SPIRIT

When I began my walk with the Lord, I did not know what "walking in the Spirit" meant. I thought that people who "walked in the Spirit" were only a few Christian leaders who could teach the Bible, had a distant, quiet personality, and operated in the supernatural gifts of the Spirit listed in 1 Corinthians 12. However, this is not the description of walking in the Spirit which Galatians 5 expresses.

This I say then, Walk in the Spirit, and ye shall not fulfil the lust of the flesh...the fruit of the Spirit is love, joy, peace, longsuffering, gentleness, goodness, faith, meekness, temperance: against such there is no law.

Galatians 5:16,22,23

Galatians 5:22 is the only place in the New Testament which uses the phrase "walk in the Spirit." According to this scripture, "walking in the Spirit" refers to not walking by the dictates of the flesh, but instead, being controlled by the Spirit within. It is choosing to walk in the fruit of the Spirit. When you receive Jesus into your heart, His life and nature come to live and abide in you. Your old life ceases to exist, and a new life begins. You receive the Spirit of God into your heart. Your spirit is recreated, born again and made new. You become a new person inside.

Second Corinthians 5:17 says, **"Therefore if any man be in Christ, he is a new creature: old things are passed away; behold, all things are become new."** Your former lifestyle and things that you did were cleansed by the blood of Jesus and were crucified with Christ.

I am crucified with Christ: nevertheless I live; yet not I, but Christ liveth in me: and the life which I now live in the flesh I live by the faith of the Son of God, who loved me, and gave himself for me.

Galatians 2:20

Jesus came into your heart and you now have His nature in you and the power of His Spirit within your spirit.

When you received Jesus, you received all of His fullness (John 1:16). That means *all* of His nature came to live inside of your recreated spirit. Knowing that you now received all of Jesus' fullness into your heart, you can't get any more of Jesus. *All* of His fruit came into your life and now you have His power to live a new life. Now instead of praying for more of Jesus to come into your life, you can pray for more of Jesus to be seen in your life and less of yourself to be what is seen.

But as many as received him, to them gave he power to become the sons of God, even to them that believe on his name.

John 1:12

It now takes faith to live and walk out His new life within you. Faith believes and accepts God's Word and acts upon it. Faith also believes and acts upon God's Word regardless of its feelings. You will find that when you choose to walk in the fruit of the Spirit, sometimes you will not feel like it. Notice in John 1:12, Jesus gives His power to us in order to help us to "become." As long as we live on this earth, we continually are "becoming" like Jesus. Second Corinthians 3:18 says we are changed from glory to glory into His image by His Spirit.

You begin to live in the Spirit the moment you are born again. You become a living spirit, alive unto God and dead to the old life. Your state of being is then "in Christ." But living in the Spirit and walking in the Spirit are two different things. This is why Paul wrote in Galatians 5:25, **"If we live in the Spirit, let us also walk in the Spirit."**

When a child is born, that child is alive but hasn't yet learned to walk. Children who are born in a family learn to walk (or conduct themselves) by the teaching and training of their parents. In a similar way, when you are born into God's family, you don't immediately start walking exactly like Jesus. It takes time to learn how to walk and then as you learn how to walk, you still are growing in your understanding. Eventually, however, people may make comments about how you walk just like your father. A small baby who is definitely alive, but who *has not made the effort to walk yet,* needs the help and encouragement of those who already can walk. This is also true spiritually speaking. No one wants to stay a baby and never grow up. This is why we must choose to walk and grow in the Spirit. **"Whoever says he abides in Him ought [as a personal debt] to walk and conduct himself in the same way in which He walked and conducted Himself"** (1 John 2:6 AMP). Jesus gives us an example of walking in the Spirit. We are to pattern our walk after Him.

"Walking in the Spirit" is to walk according to the lifestyle of Jesus, Who is now in you. It is a continual growing and changing process. You might think that walking in the fruit of the Spirit is difficult and unattainable. However, by renewing your mind to God's Word and making the decision to walk out what you are reading and studying, you can walk in His fruit and nature. Once you understand that it isn't you living your life anymore but Jesus in you with you yielding to Him, then you begin to allow Jesus to flow through you. You become conscious of His presence and you don't want to grieve His Spirit inside of you. You become more aware of the question, "What would Jesus do?" However, this comes through daily time spent with Him and then being conscious of His presence with you throughout each day.

Walking in the Spirit is a decision to daily submit your will to God's will and to obey those promptings of the Holy Spirit speaking to you. The more you obey those promptings, the stronger you'll be able to resist fleshly desires or behavior. There is a battle between the law of sin and the law of the Spirit of life in Christ Jesus. Every Christian faces this battle. This is why we have to build up our spirit man in order to subdue and conquer the law of sin. Paul, the apostle, wrote in Romans 7:15-25 that this battle within the Christian could seem frustrating and hopeless if a person did not realize the freedom that Jesus Christ gave to us. Paul wrote, **"Who will free me from my slavery…? Thank God! It has been done by Jesus Christ our Lord. He has set me free"** (verse 25 TLB).

When you realize and accept with your faith that Jesus set you free 2,000 years ago, then you can begin to enforce your freedom when sin comes to pull at your emotions, thoughts, and desires. You can begin to speak your faith – "I am delivered from the power (dominion and control) of darkness and I have been translated (and placed in) the kingdom of God's dear Son" (Col. 1:13); "I give no place to the devil" (Eph. 4:27); "I put on the Lord Jesus Christ and I do not allow or make any provision for the flesh, to fulfill any of its lusts" (Rom. 13:14); "As I have received Jesus Christ as the Lord of my life, I choose to walk in Him: rooted and built up in Him and established in the faith…" (Col. 2:6,7).

CHAPTER 2
YOU ARE A THREE-PART BEING

Once you are born again, you are a new person on the inside and you have a brand-new nature planted within you—the very nature of God Himself! The characteristics of His nature—love, joy, peace, longsuffering, gentleness, goodness, faithfulness, meekness, and self-control—are implanted within your spirit when you are born again.

At the time of your new birth, when you submit to the lordship of Jesus Christ, the growth process of these fruit and characteristics begins in your soul and body realms.

Let's first examine the fact that you are a three-part being—spirit, soul and body. **"And the very God of peace sanctify you wholly; and I pray God your whole *spirit* and *soul* and *body* be preserved blameless unto the coming of our Lord Jesus Christ"** (1 Thessalonians 5:23). You are a *spirit*, you have a *soul*, and you live in a *body*. The part that everyone sees is the body. However, the real you is your *spirit* man.

When I was first born again, I did not realize there was a differentiation in the spirit and soul, because many times these terms are used interchangeably. However, in the New Testament, there are scriptures that help us better understand, such as the one I just quoted from 1 Thessalonians. Hebrews 4:12 tells us that **"... the word of God is quick, and powerful, and sharper than any twoedged sword, piercing even to the *dividing asunder of soul and spirit*, and of the joints and marrow, and is a discerner of the thoughts and intents of the heart."**

The Spirit

Colossians 3:10 refers to your *spirit* man as "the new man." **"And have put on the new man, which is renewed in knowledge after the image of him that created him."** Ephesians 4:24 also refers to your spirit man as "the new man." **"And that ye put on *the new man*, which after God is created in righteousness and true holiness."** First Peter 3:4 calls your spirit man "the hidden man of the heart." **"But let it be *the hidden man of the heart*, in that which is not corruptible, even the ornament of a meek and quiet spirit, which is in the sight of God of great price."**

This part of us—our spirit man—is "hidden within us" but is as real as what we can see with our natural eyes. This is the part that God breathed into Adam when He created him and that He breathes into us (Genesis 2:7). (Note: Animals do not have a spirit. They have a body and reasoning faculties, along with emotional responses, but no spirit. Only human beings possess a spirit.) Our spirit is the part of us that only God can fill and fulfill. This is the part of us that is born again, as Jesus put it in John 3:3-8. Animals cannot be born again because they do not have a spirit; only people can be born again.

The Soul

The *soul* is that part of us which also cannot be seen but is very real—our thinking faculties and reasoning, along with our emotions or feelings, desires and our will. For humans, both the *spirit* and the *soul* will live eternally after the body dies. In the resurrection from the dead, those who have died in Christ will receive a glorified body. All people will live forever, either in heaven or in hell.

In Luke 16:19-31, Jesus tells the story of a certain rich man and a beggar named Lazarus. (Note: This is not a parable, or He would have said so. Instead, Jesus spoke of this event as an actual happening.) Lazarus, the beggar, laid daily at the rich man's gate, very sickly, hoping for some crumbs from the rich man's table. One day both the rich man and Lazarus died. The rich man went to hell, and Lazarus went to Abraham's bosom (a place of paradise where the righteous went until Jesus Christ came to raise them to heaven).

Though his body was dead, the rich man could still see, feel and know pain and sorrow. He saw Lazarus afar off, beyond the gulf that separated them. The place of eternal torment and fire that he was in caused him to cry out to try to get Abraham's attention. Abraham heard him but could not help him because it was too late. Notice, the man's *thinking faculties, emotions and will* to get out of where he was, were still very much alive. The soul and the spirit live forever.

One of the torments of hell, besides being a lake of eternal fire and brimstone, will be that people there will know about others who go to heaven but they won't be able to get to them. Also, they will be able to remember the times they rejected God's Spirit convicting them on earth and the people who tried to warn them. They will know those they influenced to go to hell. Hell will not be a big party like some have jokingly said. It will be the worst horror a person could ever imagine, forever. Thank God we can escape hell and go to heaven.

Renew the Mind

Many who receive Jesus into their hearts fail to understand that unless they renew their minds, they will not be able to resist the devil and walk the Christian life successfully. Realizing that we are spirit, soul and body helps us to see why some people who are born again still struggle walking in the Spirit. The soul has to be renewed daily to God's Word and His Word changes our way of thinking and acting.

Proverbs 23:7 says, **"For as he thinketh in his heart, so is**

he." In other words, whatever you think about, you will act out. That's why it is so important to control our thoughts and not allow them to think wildly on just anything that comes along. We can choose to think good thoughts and reject wrong thoughts. God's Word is a plumb line to keep our lives in right balance if we put it into our minds daily.

Man is a Three-Part Being: Sprit, Soul and Body

Spirit – Heart of Man

Soul – Mind (Intellect)

Emotions

Will

Body – Outward Shell

The Body

First Corinthians 6:19,20 tells us that as Christians our body is the temple of the Holy Ghost which is in us, which we have of God, and we are not our own. We've been bought with the price of Jesus' blood, so we belong to Him and we are to glorify Him in our spirit, body and soul.

Romans 12:1,2 tells us the way we present our *bodies* to God to glorify Him is by renewing our minds. Thus, we won't become conformed to the way the world around us thinks and acts, but we will be conformed to what Scripture says. No wonder God told the Jewish people to *meditate* His Word day and night, for then they would observe to *do* it, be blessed and yield fruit even in difficult times. (See Psalm 1:1-3; Joshua 1:8.) Thus, meditation—what we think about—will produce action or will be acted out.

Ephesians 4:23 says, **"And be renewed in the spirit of your mind."** The Greek word for *renewal* is *ananeoo*, which means that the whole course of life now flows in a different direction.[1] Putting God's Word in our minds daily causes us to walk in a different direction than the world around us.

Jesus said in John 8:31,32, **"If ye continue in my word, then are ye my disciples indeed; and ye shall know the truth, and the truth shall make you free."** Many people only quote the last part of this scripture, but freedom from the dictates or control of the flesh nature and the ways of this world come from *continuing to know God's Word.* It's not enough to hear the truth preached one time that Jesus has set us free. We must continue in the truth to stay free. That means a daily time of putting God's Word in your life. Then you can walk in freedom and walk in the Spirit.

Even when you don't think anything is happening in you as a result of reading a portion of your Bible each day, it is. The Bible is not like any other book. The words in it are spiritually empowered to change and keep us. (See John 6:63; Proverbs 4:22.)

We can put God's Word in us by the following ways:

1. Hearing God's Word (Romans 10:17). By attending church,

listening to teaching on radio, TV, or cassettes, or reading God's Word out loud to yourself, you *hear* God's Word.

2. Reading God's Word (Revelation 1:3). Have a daily Bible reading time.

3. Studying God's Word (2 Timothy 2:15). Study Scripture and read good teaching books on different subjects.

4. Memorizing and meditating upon God's Word (Psalm 119:9,11; 1:2,3). Find scriptures to memorize on different subjects such as peace, healing, love, restoration, freedom, power, etc.

5. Praying or speaking God's Word over your life (Joshua 1:8). Pray the scriptures over your life that you want to rule in your life.

6. Praising God with His Word by singing scriptures. Scriptural songs also build up your spirit man.

God's words are spirit and they are life (John 6:63). His Word contains the power of the Spirit of God to change your life.

If you walk in the Spirit and are led by God's Word, you will be able to live the abundant life that Jesus has provided (John 10:10). The fruit of His Spirit will begin to grow in you. The desire to gratify your flesh will decrease, while increasingly, you will desire to submit your flesh to your born-again spirit, which is now dominated by the Holy Spirit and God's Word.

Endotes

[1] Finis Jennings Dake. *Dake's Annotated Reference Bible*, Lawrenceville, GA: Dake Bible Sales, Inc., 1963, 1991, p. 210.

CHAPTER 3
THE FLESH VS. THE SPIRIT

As we examine verses 19-21 of Galatians, chapter 5, we see that the church in Galatia had the same problems toward sin that many people in the Church have today—the lust of the flesh.

Now the works of the flesh [also referred to as "lusts" in verses 16,17] **are manifest, which are these; Adultery, fornication, uncleanness, lasciviousness,**
Idolatry, witchcraft, hatred, variance, emulations, wrath, strife, seditions, heresies,
Envyings, murders, drunkenness, revellings, and such like: of the which I tell you before, as I have also told you in time past, that they which do such things shall not inherit the kingdom of God.

Let's examine some of Vine, Unger, Dake, Richards and Webster's descriptions of the lusts of the flesh:

1. Adultery - *Moichos* in the Greek means one who has intercourse with the spouse of another.[2] *Unger's Bible Dictionary* describes *adultery* as the willful violation of the marriage contract by either party, through sexual intercourse with a third party. The divine provision was that the husband and wife should become "one flesh," each being held sacred to the other.[3] *Webster's Dictionary* defines *adultery* as voluntary sexual intercourse between a married man and a woman not his wife, or between a married woman and a man not her husband.[4]

2. Fornication - *Porneia* in the Greek means illicit sexual intercourse.[5] *Unger's Bible Dictionary* states that at the present

time, *adultery* is the term used of such an act when the person is married, *fornication* when unmarried. *Fornication* may be defined as lewdness of an unmarried person of either sex. Its prohibition rests on the ground that it discourages marriage, leaves the education and care of children insecure, depraves and defiles the mind more than any other vice, and thus such a person is unfit for the Kingdom of God (1 Corinthians 6:9). Our Lord forbids the thoughts that lead to it (Matthew 5:28).[6] *Webster's Dictionary* defines *fornication* as voluntary sexual intercourse, generally forbidden by law, between an unmarried woman and a man; any unlawful sexual intercourse, including adultery.[7]

3. Uncleanness - *Akatharsia* in the Greek means impure; physical and moral defilement.[8] Dake says this includes sodomy, homosexuality, lesbianism, pederasty, bestiality, and all other forms of sexual perversion.[9] (Note: Incest would also be included in this category.) *Richards' Expository Dictionary of the Bible* says, "The spiritually sensitive realized that uncleanness was a matter of the heart and not simply a ritual issue."[10] *Webster's Dictionary* defines uncleanness as morally impure; unchaste, obscene, or vile.[11]

4. Lasciviousness - *Aselgeia* in the Greek means licentiousness, an absence of restraint, wantonness and indecency.[12] Webster says lasciviousness is characterized by or expressing lust or lewdness; wanton, tending to excite lustful desires.[13] (This would include pornography and any TV, videos, magazines, the Internet, or places where sexual lust is fostered.) Webster defines *wanton* as sexually loose or unrestrained.[14] *Webster's New World Dictionary* states that licentiousness is disregarding accepted rules and standards, morally unrestrained, especially in sexual activity.[15]

5. Idolatry - *Eidololateia* in the Greek means primarily a phantom or likeness or an idea.[16] *Richards* defines idolatry as anything that one may shape for use as an object of worship.[17] Webster defines *idolatry* as excessive devotion to or reverence for some person or thing. Idolatry is anything that occupies your mind more than God. It replaces a passion for God. (This could include good things such as romantic partners, family, sports,

work, hobbies—anything which becomes one's object of affection or devotion more than God.)[18]

6. Witchcraft - *Pharmakeia* in the Greek means medicine, drugs, spells. In sorcery, the use of drugs, whether simple or potent, was generally accompanied by incantations (or words spoken) and appeals to occult powers, with the provision of various charms, amulets (bracelets or necklaces, etc.) professedly designed to keep the applicant or patient from the attention and power of demons, but actually to impress (or strongly influence) this person with the mysterious resources and powers of the sorcerer.[19] As Christians we are encouraged to avoid anything, other than God, that would have a controlling influence upon our minds, such as drugs, alcohol, psychics, hypnosis, etc.

We are to keep our lives in submission to God and to His written Word and not allow attitudes of rebellion, such as exist in the world around us. First Samuel 15:23 says, **"For rebellion is as the sin of witchcraft, and stubbornness is as iniquity and idolatry. . . ."** Rebellion is a rejection of God and is in direct opposition to the plans and purposes of God.

Witchcraft is a rejection of God and His ways. It seeks guidance inspired by the devil, since he was the first to reject and resist God and seeks to plant that attitude in mankind. Stubbornness is as iniquity and idolatry because it demands its own way and refuses to submit to God's way. Idolatry exalts a thing, person, idea, opinion, or belief above God. Stubbornness exalts one's own opinion and direction above God. It is the worship of self, and it is idolatry and sin according to the Scripture.

7. Hatred - *Echthra* in the Greek means having enmity.[20] Webster defines *hatred* as to have strong dislike or ill will for; loathe, despise, to dislike or wish to avoid; shrink from; feeling great dislike or aversion with persons; bearing malice; looking down upon someone with great contempt.[21]

8. Variance - *Eris* in the Greek means to cut apart; divide in two; strife.[22] Webster defines variance as an action; disagreement; quarrel; dispute.[23] God hasn't called His people to separate others

they influence, but to be reconcilers and peacemakers.

9. Emulations - *Zelos* in the Greek means to provoke jealousies and envy.[24] Webster defines envy as feeling of discontent and ill will because of another person's advantages, desire for some advantage another has; resentful dislike of another who has something that one desires.[25]

10.Wrath - *Thumos* in the Greek means hot anger and passion; the strongest of all passions; an agitated condition of the feelings; an outburst of anger from inward indignation.[26]

Unger's Bible Dictionary describes *wrath* as turbulent commotion, the boiling agitation of the feelings, either presently to subside and disappear or else settle down into *orge* (Greek), a more abiding and settled habit of mind with the purpose of revenge.[27] Webster states that *wrath* is intense anger, rage, fury.[28] Christians who lose their temper and physically respond by attacking people with words or physical harm are abusive and need to submit their spirit to the fruit of self-control with the help of the Holy Spirit.

11.Strife - *Eritheia* in the Greek means contention, enmity, rivalry; self-will being the underlying idea.[29] Webster defines strife as vying with one another; contention or competition; quarreling; to bitterly struggle; conflict; dissent, disagreement, or lack of concord. (See also *discontent*, p. 402)[30]

12. Seditions - *Dichostasia* in the Greek means divisions; parties and factions; popular disorder; stirring up strife in religion, government, home, or any other place.[31] Vine describes *seditions* as standing apart.[32] *Unger's Bible Dictionary* says that *dichostasia* is generally used in the sense of rebellion, insurrection, standing apart.[33]

13. Heresies - *Hairesis* in the Greek means a choosing or choice; an opinion, especially a self-willed opinion, which is substituted for submission to the power of truth and leads to division and the formation of sects; such erroneous opinions are frequently the outcome of personal preference or the prospect of advantage.[34] Webster defines *heresies* as the rejection of a belief that is a part of church dogma or doctrine; any opinion opposed to official or established views or doctrines.[35]

14. Envyings - *Phthonos* in the Greek means the feeling of displeasure produced by witnessing or hearing of the advantage or prosperity of others; an evil sense is attached to this word. The distinction between jealousy or emulations (Greek – *zeloi*) and envy (Greek – *phthoni*) is that envy desires to deprive another of what he has, while jealousy desires to have the same or the same sort of thing for itself.[36] Both are sin!

15. Murders - *Phonoi* in the Greek means to kill, to spoil or mar the happiness of another; hatred.[37] Webster defines *murder* as the unlawful and malicious or premeditated killing of a human being by another; also any killing done while committing some other felony, as rape or robbery; to spoil or mar.[38]

16. Drunkenness - *Methuo* in the Greek means to be drunk with wine; intoxicated.[39] Webster defines *drunkenness* as habitual, intemperate drinking of liquor; to be overcome by alcoholic liquor to the point of losing control over one's faculties; intoxicated.[40]

17. Revellings - *Komos* in the Greek means the concomitant and consequence of drunkenness; riot.[41] Dake defines *revellings* as rioting; lascivious (that which excites lustful desires) and boisterous (noisy, rough, lively, coarse and unmannerly) feastings, with obscene music and other sinful activities; pleasures; carousings (drinking parties).[42] Webster defines *revel* as to make merry, being noisily festive;[43] *rebel* as a person who resists any authority or controls[44] and *riot* as wild or violent disorder; to live in a wild, loose manner; to engage in unrestrained revelry.[45]

We must realize that we're in a battle spiritually. Galatians 5:17 says, **"For the flesh lusteth** [or is at war with] **against the Spirit, and the Spirit against the flesh."** Paul recognized this same conflict in himself:

> **But I discern in my bodily members [in the sensitive appetites and wills of the flesh] a different law (rule of action) at war against the law of my mind (my reason) and making me a prisoner to the law of sin that dwells in my bodily organs [in the sensitive appetites and wills of the flesh].**
>
> **Romans 7:23** AMP

15

He goes on to ask himself, **"Who will release and deliver me from [the shackles of] this body of death? O thank God! [He will!] through Jesus Christ (the Anointed One) our Lord!"** (vv. 24,25 AMP). Paul goes on to explain in Romans, chapter 8, how we walk free. When we walk after the Spirit, we set our minds on the things of the Spirit, not on the things of the flesh. This produces life and peace in our lives. **"To be carnally minded is death; but to be spiritually minded is life and peace"** (Romans 8:6). The more we set our minds to think according to God's Word, the more we will live in abundant life and in the peace of God. Where there is a lack of God's Word, there will be a lack of abundant life and peace.

God has provided what we need to overcome the temptations and tests of the flesh, but we must *use the keys* to enforce our freedom and walk in it. (Note: Jesus was tempted and tested in all points like we are, yet He was without sin (Hebrews 2:18). He overcame the devil in the wilderness by speaking scriptures He had memorized (Matthew, chapter 4). He said, **"It is written,"** to each temptation that Satan brought.).

Second Peter 1:4 says that we've been given the Word of God to partake of the divine nature of Jesus and to escape the corruption that's in the world through lust. By getting God's Word into your heart and mind, you *will be able to escape the lusts of the flesh* and walk in the Spirit's control.

It boils down to choices that we make. It takes a conscious effort on our part to choose to obey God's Word in regard to walking in the fruit of the Spirit and not letting our flesh do whatever it feels justified to do.

In Joshua 24:14,15, Joshua spoke to the entire congregation, urging them to make a decision as to whom they were going to serve—God Almighty or the gods of their fathers. The gods of their fathers meant they would do whatever their flesh craved to do. Serving God Almighty meant they would obey His commandments and hearken to whatever He said. Obeying God meant life and blessing. Serving the gods of their fathers meant death and cursing.

In Deuteronomy 30:19,20, God gave them the same choice and said that if they would love Him, obey Him and cleave to Him, He would give them length of days and both they and their seed would live. Joshua stated his decision in Joshua 24:15: **"...as for me and my house, we will serve the Lord."**

God still gives us, and our seed, the same choice today— blessing or cursing, death or life. You choose life and blessing when you choose not to serve your flesh but to live by the Spirit and obey His Word. James 1:22-25 tells us that it is the doer of God's Word who is blessed. The Christian who is a *hearer only* is deceiving himself (or herself). Choose to be a doer of the Word of God. Choose to walk in the Spirit. It is up to you to choose to serve and submit or yield to the dictates of your flesh, or to serve, submit or yield to the Spirit of God.

Now let's look at how to walk in the Spirit and bring forth the new nature that is within us.

First of all, submitting to the lordship of Jesus daily and abiding in His Word will enable us to exemplify the life of the Spirit.

Secondly, the deeper your revelation is of Jesus (or the more you know and learn of Jesus) through the Word, prayer and obedience, the greater will be the manifestation of His fruit in your life!

Thirdly, you are in a growth process. You are not fully developed. Like clay in a potter's hands, you're being molded. Don't become frustrated or complacent in your growth or decide you don't want to grow anymore. Keep yourself in a yielded position to God. Continue to be hungry and thirsty spiritually.

Endotes

[2] W. E. Vine. *An Expository Dictionary of New Testament Words*, Nashville, TN: Thomas Nelson Publishers, pp. 24-25.

[3] *Unger's Bible Dictionary*. Chicago, IL: Moody Bible Institute, 1957, 1961, 1966, p. 29.

[4] *Webster's New World Dictionary,* Second College Ed., New York, NY: Simon & Schuster, 1982, p. 19.

[5] Vine, p. 455.

[6] Unger, p. 378.

[7] Webster, p. 549.

[8] Vine, pp. 1178, 1179.

[9] Dake, p. 207.

[10] Lawrence O. Richards. *Richards' Expository Dictionary of the Bible,* 1985, p. 170.
[11] Webster, p. 1544.
[12] Vine, p. 640.
[13] Webster, p. 795.
[14] Ibid., p. 1600.
[15] Ibid., p. 815.
[16] Vine, p. 574.
[17] Richards, p. 349.
[18] Webster, p. 697.
[19] Vine, pp. 1064, 1065.
[20] Ibid., p. 528.
[21] Webster, p. 641.
[22] Vine, p. 1195.
[23] Webster, p. 1570.
[24] Vine, pp. 603, 604.
[25] Webster, p. 468.
[26] Vine, p. 1251.
[27] Unger, p. 1174.
[28] Webster, p. 1641.
[29] Vine, p. 1095.
[30] Webster, p. 1410.
[31] Dake, p. 207.
[32] Vine, p. 336.
[33] Unger, p. 991.
[34] Vine, p. 547.
[35] Webster, p. 656.
[36] Vine, p. 367.
[37] Dake, p. 207.
[38] Webster, p. 936.
[39] Vine, pp. 333, 334.
[40] Webster, p. 430.
[41] Vine, p. 965.
[42] Dake, p. 207.
[43] Webster, p. 1216.
[44] Ibid., p. 1183.
[45] Ibid., p. 1227.

CHAPTER 4
THE GROWTH PROCESS

God's will is growth. Every living thing is growing. Living things either grow bigger, older, wiser, smarter, better and stronger, or they stop growing and begin to die. We cannot simply reach a point and stand still. God wants us to grow throughout our lives spiritually. He wants us to grow stronger as the years go by so that we are more effective for the Kingdom of God. He desires for us to grow and multiply in fruitfulness (John 15:5).

A scientist once said that thorns on rose bushes are actually undeveloped roses. Personally, I believe that in the beginning, when God created the earth, there were no thorns on rose bushes. I believe that the thorns came after Adam and Eve sinned.

We can see the analogy of the rose bush in the Christian Kingdom. While many Christians go through the growth process and develop into beautiful roses, some do not. Instead, they become thorns in the Body of Christ, always sticking and hurting people, or having to be dealt with carefully so they won't get upset or hurt another person. We can see how vital the growth process of the Christian really is!

Learning to walk in the Spirit requires a process of time. It will not occur within a day or even within a month, even though all nine fruit of the Spirit of God were implanted within you as "seed" when you were born again. **"Being born again, not of corruptible seed, but of incorruptible, by the word of God, which liveth and abideth for ever"** (1 Peter 1:23).

Just as a baby is born into this natural world with all the muscles and body parts that an adult has, he or she is undeveloped. So it

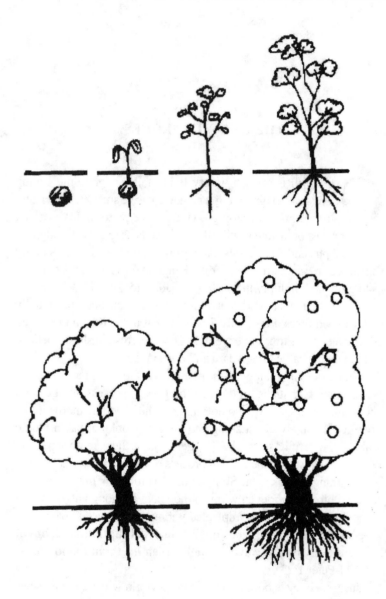

is with a spiritual birth. Spiritually speaking, you have all the spiritual muscles (the faith, Romans 12:3; the fruit, Galatians 5:22,23; the fullness of Jesus' life, John 1:16; and the power, John 1:12) when you are born into the Kingdom of God. However, all of these are undeveloped. Your submission to the growth process will determine how strong you become and how effective you will be in changing the world around you with the Gospel.

As the diagram on page **20** shows, there are several stages of the seed's growth. In this chapter we will compare these growth stages of fruitfulness with the growth of a fruit tree:

1. The seed.
2. The tender sprout.
3. The young seedling.
4. The tree with leaves.
5. The tree with blossoms.
6. The tree with fruit.

Seed needs nurturing for it to germinate. If you do not nurture it, it will become stagnant (dull, motionless, or inactive). In the same way, we must nurture the seed of God's Word in our lives so that it will grow. First Peter 2:2 says, **"Desire the sincere milk of the word, that ye may grow thereby."** Begin a daily time of reading God's Word. Nurturing also happens spiritually by becoming planted in a church body where you hear sound teaching regularly. It's similar to a plant nursery where plants are protected from outside elements that could destroy them (Psalm 92:12-14). Nurturing the seed also involves daily watering and proper lighting which come from the Word of God and the Holy Spirit being given free flow in our lives.

The Word of God—which is the seed—is first solidly planted in the good soil of your heart when you receive Jesus. As the seed begins to grow, your roots must extend deep into the soil, establishing your heart. **"As ye have therefore received Christ Jesus the Lord, *so walk ye in him: Rooted* and *built up in him*, and *stablished* in the faith, as ye have been taught, abounding** therein with thanksgiving" (Colossians 2:6,7).

The Japanese cultivate exquisite miniature trees called bonsai trees. Although perfectly proportioned, their total size is dwarfed by deliberately clipping their roots. Because of this special clipping, these trees will never grow to their full size, even though they are mature in every other way.

God doesn't want your roots to be cut or dwarfed. He wants our roots to go down deep into the soil of His Word and to spring forth in the length and the height and the depth of His love so that you may grow into the fullness of maturity in Jesus.

For he shall be like a tree planted by the waters that spreads out its roots by the river; and *it shall not see and fear when heat comes*; but its leaf shall be green. It shall not be anxious and full of care in the year of drought, nor shall it cease yielding fruit.

Jeremiah 17:8 AMP

The heat could be offenses, obstacles and pressures that come against you. Do you see it and fear, or do you walk through with God's divine peace? We are the ones who cut our own roots and stop our growth process by taking offenses, separating ourselves from the church (our nurturing place), allowing ourselves to be overwhelmed and overcome by the obstacles and pressures, or just letting go of and neglecting what we know helps us spiritually. Hosea 4:6 says God's people are destroyed because of a lack of knowledge (not pursuing to know the Word), or because they reject the instruction of God's Word, or because they simply forget it.

The seed, through nourishment from the Word of God, germinates into the first stage of growth and brings forth a young, tender sprout. The young seedling can be easily bruised, injured, offended or hindered. Make a decision to love God's Word and release offenses. Psalm 119:165 says, **"Great peace have they which love thy law** [the Word]: **and nothing shall offend them."**

"A bruised reed He will not break, and a smoldering (dimly burning) wick He will not quench. . ." (Matthew 12:20 AMP). *The Living Bible* says, **"He does not crush the weak, or**

22

quench the smallest hope. . . ." Jesus understands where we are in our growth and extends His grace to us when we are weak.

Paul was offended, reproached and persecuted, but he said that God's grace was sufficient to carry him and that in the midst of his weakness, God's strength was made perfect (or matured) in him.

And he said unto me, My grace is sufficient for thee: for my strength is made perfect in weakness. Most gladly therefore will I rather glory in my infirmities, that the power of Christ may rest upon me.

2 Corinthians 12:9

God seems to take joy in showing Himself strong when we are weak and have exhausted our own natural strength. (A reminder to Christians is that just as Jesus is tender and forbearing with us, we must be tender and forbearing with one another throughout the various stages of Christian growth.)

The seedling will mature into a young tree as it is affectionately cared for and properly nourished. Make sure you guard and care for your spirit man. Let your roots extend deep into the soil. The growth of a Christian happens as he receives daily nourishment from the Word of God, stays planted in a church where he is loved and accepted and hears regular teaching of the truths of God's Word.

The depth of the Christian's roots refers not only to a knowledge of the Word, but also to an understanding or application of it, enabling him or her to become a doer of the Word. **"But be ye doers of the word, and not hearers only, deceiving your own selves"** (James 1:22). The more you know and understand, the more responsible you are to walk it out in your life. (Those are strong words!)

As the leaves spring forth upon the young tree, they look pretty and they provide shade, but they cannot be eaten for nourishment or used for any other reason. As a child of God, you must go on to perfection (maturity) if you are to be mightily used of God in providing His nourishment and truths to others. In Mark 11, Jesus looked for fruit on a fig tree that had many pretty leaves. It was deceptive, because from a distance it looked like it should be full of fruit, but when Jesus got close to it, it had no fruit.

Jesus is looking for fruit in our lives. He doesn't want us to look fruitful from a distance but be barren when one actually gets a closer look at us. We must go on to maturity and grow in Him. The closer other people get to you, the more it will become evident whether or not you are simply a great talker or you actually desire Jesus to flow through your attitudes and actions.

As the young tree matures, blossoms will come forth. The blossoms are always beautiful, and they will give off a fragrance, attracting the attention of others. So it is in a Christian's life. Your blossoms will cause others to be drawn to the sweet aroma of Jesus Christ! The more spiritual victories you win, the more you create an atmosphere around your life that others are drawn to, desiring to know what you know.

Now thanks be unto God, which always causeth us to triumph in Christ, and maketh manifest the savour of his knowledge by us in every place.

For we are unto God a sweet savour of Christ, in them that are saved, and in them that perish.

2 Corinthians 2:14,15

Blossoms indicate that fruit is on the way. Tiny fruit begins to protrude through the blossoms. Finally the blossoms totally disappear, but the fruit remains. Although the fruit may begin small, in a process of time, it will become large and luscious. As the fruit becomes mature for eating, people will see the fruit coming from your life. Your witness will draw them closer to Jesus.

People will seek you out for wisdom and counsel, partaking of your love and gentleness, and they will gain insight in how to apply God's Word in their lives.

Factors in Growth

There are several other factors in the Christian's growth which you need to recognize, particularly the factors of soil, water, light, and season (or timing).

Soil

First, a humble and surrendered heart makes good soil in which to plant God's Word. Secondly, a heart that hungers and thirsts for God will be filled (Matthew 5:6). Because your vessel is pouring out each day, it needs to be filled again each day. God's Word and His Holy Spirit are the nutrients used to germinate the seeds of God's nature implanted within you when you are born again.

As newborn babes, desire the sincere milk of the word, that ye may grow thereby.

1 Peter 2:2

When most believers are first born again, they hunger for the Word of God. After a season, however, sometimes because of the pressures and cares of daily life and a lack of time spent in the presence of the Lord, they slack off in their desire for God's Word and allow their hearts to become hardened. To keep from becoming hardened, Scripture says we must keep an attitude of hunger like a newborn babe who hungers to be fed. (Note: A newborn's stomach is small and cannot take in large amounts so he has to eat often.) Matthew 4:4 says, **"Man shall not live by bread alone, but by every word that proceedeth out of the mouth of God."**

In the same way we need food, we need to purpose in our hearts, as an act of our own will, to seek the Lord daily through His Word, through prayer and fellowship. Through special times spent with Him we grow. The Word of God says, **"Sow to yourselves in righteousness, reap in mercy; break up your fallow ground: for it is time to seek the Lord, till he come and rain righteousness upon you"** (Hosea 10:12).

Has the ground of your heart become fallow? *Fallow ground*

is ground that has been plowed up at one time, but because it has not been planted or used, it hardens. It is unproductive. In order to have seed planted in it, it must be plowed up again. We break up or plow up our heart by purposely deciding to humble ourselves, yield our heart and will to God and seek Him.

Water

Another necessary ingredient for growth—water—will help keep the ground of your heart soft and pliable in God's hands.

First, God says that there must be a repentant heart before the water or times of refreshing will come to your spirit. A *repentant heart* or *attitude* is a heart that is sensitive to the conviction and working of the Holy Spirit. A person who is quick to repent of any wrong attitude or action is a person who can receive the rivers of the Spirit working through their life.

So repent (change your mind and purpose); turn around and return [to God], that your sins may be erased (blotted out, wiped clean), that times of refreshing (of recovering from the effects of heat, of reviving with fresh air) may come from the presence of the Lord.

Acts 3:19 AMP

The river of God's Spirit is an essential ingredient for the Christian's growth.

Jesus said:

If any man thirst, let him come unto me, and drink.

He that believeth on me, as the scripture hath said, out of his belly shall flow rivers of living water.

But this spake he of the Spirit, which they that believe on him should receive: for the Holy Ghost was not yet given; because that Jesus was not yet glorified.

John 7:37-39

Ephesians 5:18 commands us to **"be filled with the Spirit."** The connotation of this scripture indicates that we must stay being filled on a regular basis. Ask the Lord to fill you with His Spirit. Believe He fills you when you ask (Luke 11:9-13). Then yield to

Him to pray and worship on a daily basis (Ephesians 5:19).

As the rains of the Spirit fall in your life, refreshing comes to the soil of your heart and stimulates your spirit. **"Ask ye of the Lord rain in the time of the latter rain, so the Lord shall make bright clouds, and give them showers of rain, to every one grass in the field"** (Zechariah 10:1).

Worshipping the Lord brings us the rain of His Spirit. I'm not only speaking of singing songs in a church service; I'm speaking of being a worshipper daily with your entire life. **"And it shall be that whoso of the families of the earth *shall not go up* to Jerusalem *to worship* the King, the Lord of hosts, *upon them there shall be no rain"*** (Zechariah 14:17 AMP). Zechariah went so far as to say that if a person refuses to worship the Lord, he will receive no rain.

In the New Testament, Jesus told the woman at the well that God the Father doesn't require us to worship in Jerusalem or on a certain mountain. Since God is a Spirit, He seeks true worshippers who will worship Him in spirit and in truth. Worship is not based upon a place but upon the attitude of the heart.

In Matthew 15:9 Jesus said some people worship Him in vain with their lips but their heart is far from Him. To worship Him in spirit, our hearts must be connected to our words. To worship Him in truth, our worship is not a performance or an attempt to impress other people, but we worship Him out of true sincerity of heart. Our praise and worship should be motivated out of love for God from our heart, soul, mind and strength (Mark 12:30). That involves your heart, your emotions, your mind and your body freely worshipping God according to Scripture. The psalmist understood worship and gives us God's pattern of expressing our praise and worship to God.

No wonder God seeks worshippers like this! He has their full attention. Worshipping in truth is worshipping according to the truth of God's Word. God is pleased when we are doers of His Word. Worship brings the rain of God's Spirit into a believer's life. Ephesians 5:19 says that one way to be filled with God's Spirit is to sing and make melody in your heart to the Lord.

God's Word also acts as water, cleansing and refreshing us. Jesus Himself sanctifies and cleanses us with the washing of water by His Word. **"Now ye are clean through the word which I have spoken unto you"** (John 15:3). **"That he might sanctify and cleanse it with** *the washing of water by the word"* (Ephesians 5:26). As you study the Word of God and allow it to dwell in you richly, like water it will cleanse you and stimulate growth in your life.

Isaiah compares God's Word to the rain and snow in chapter 55, verses 10, 11 AMP:

> **For** *as the rain and snow come down* **from the heavens, and return not there again, but water the earth and make it bring forth and sprout, that it may give seed to the sower and bread to the eater,**
> *So shall My word be that goes forth out of My mouth: it shall not return to Me void [without producing any effect, useless], but it shall accomplish that which I please and purpose, and it shall prosper in the thing for which I sent it.*

Continually allow God's Spirit and His Word to water the seeds of His nature planted within your heart so your branches will grow and stay spiritually healthy.

Light

Plants (or seeds) must have light to cause them to flourish in abundant vitality. Again, the Word of God produces light and the fellowship of other Christians creates an atmosphere of growth for a stable walk in Christ Jesus.

Psalm 119:105 says, **"Thy word is a lamp unto my feet, and a light unto my path."** People who are committed to a time of daily reading of God's Word will be able to hear His guidance more easily. No Word input equals walking in darkness, and it's easy to stumble when you're walking in the dark.

As you study God's Word, it will bring you light and make you aware of His plan and purpose for your life, because He has a unique, divine plan for you. Don't settle for unclear direction. Seek God's Word for His plan for you. Ask Him to enlighten your understanding that His plan for you may become clear.

[For I always pray to] the God of our Lord Jesus Christ, the Father of glory, that He may grant you a spirit of wisdom and revelation [of insight into mysteries and secrets] in the [deep and intimate] knowledge of Him,

By *having the eyes of your heart flooded with light, so that you can know and understand the hope to which He has called you,* **and how rich is His glorious inheritance in the saints (His set-apart ones).**

Ephesians 1:17,18 AMP

Can Light and Darkness Have Fellowship?

Christians often desire to witness to their former friends who are still in darkness. Although it is important to witness to those in darkness (in Satan's domain), it is essential that you discontinue your close fellowship with those who are still in darkness. **"Be ye not unequally yoked together with unbelievers: for what fellowship hath righteousness with unrighteoussness? and** *what communion hath light with darkness?"* (2 Corinthians 6:14).

Remember, habitual fellowship with someone can affect you. Proverbs 13:20 says, **"He that walketh with wise men shall be wise: but a companion of fools shall be destroyed."** You can share with people without fellowshipping with them in their darkness.

Continued fellowship with those in darkness has caused some Christians to fall by the wayside and be shipwrecked in their faith. First Corinthians 15:33 tells us not to be deceived, for wrong or evil associations will corrupt good morals. Ask the Lord for Christian friends who will be able to help you grow. As you grow, you'll become stronger spiritually and will be able to stand firm around unbelievers, bringing them to the Lord without their pulling you down.

Timing

Psalm 31:15 NIV says, **"My times are in your hands."** Timing or "due season" is also essential to the fulfillment or maturity of fruit, both in the natural and in the Christian's life. Ecclesiastes 3:11 says that God makes all things beautiful in *His* time. Remember, a seed does not become a tree overnight. Everything that lives takes time to grow and mature. Even after much growth, we need time for seasoning or ripening.

Galatians 6:9 AMP says:

> **And let us not lose heart and grow weary and faint in acting nobly and doing right, for in due time and at the appointed season we shall reap, if we do not loosen and relax our courage and faint.**

I recall one time years ago when we were newly married. I went to the grocery store to buy groceries. I saw a specially priced batch of bananas so I selected some that looked perfect—totally free of spots and bruises, although they were still quite green. When I got home, I decided to try one. I had to get a knife to pry the peel open. I could hardly separate the peel from the banana. Needless to say, it tasted awful. It was quite obvious that the banana needed more time to ripen to full maturity.

That's the way it is with Christians. We don't become mature the moment we are born again. Maturity will surely come, but it will take a process of time. You can't rush growth, but you can learn to remain in peace during each season of growth and be thankful. Think about it this way. God is growing you as an oak tree that will stand the tests of storms and strong winds that may come. However, you'll have to be willing to do what your flesh doesn't want to do at times in order to become stronger.

Philippians 3:11-16 AMP says:

> **That if possible I may attain to the [spiritual and moral] resurrection [that lifts me] out from among the dead [even while in the body].**
>
> **Not that I have now attained [this ideal], or have already been made perfect, but I press on to lay hold of (grasp) and make my own, that for which Christ Jesus (the Messiah) has laid hold of me and made me His own.**
>
> **I do not consider, brethren, that I have captured and made it my own [yet]; but one thing I do [it is my one aspiration]: forgetting what lies behind and straining forward to what lies ahead.**
>
> **I press on toward the goal to win the [supreme and heavenly] prize to which God in Christ Jesus is calling us upward.**
>
> *So let those [of us] who are spiritually mature and full-grown have this mind and hold these convictions;* **and if in any respect you have a different attitude of mind, God will make that clear to you also.**
>
> **Only let us** *hold true to what we have already attained and walk and order our lives by that.*

Do not be so satisfied with the growth you have attained thus far that you don't desire to grow anymore. Keep the fire of God in your life by pressing forward (making effort) to know Him more and be used as a vessel to share this Gospel of the Kingdom with others.

My husband has said that perfection (or maturity) can be attained at each stage of growth in a person's life – it's not just a goal at the end of life. **"But grow in grace (undeserved favor, spiritual strength) and recognition and knowledge and understanding of our Lord and Savior Jesus Christ (the Messiah)..."** (2 Peter 3:18 AMP).

Understanding that you are in a growth process sets you free from comparing yourself to others and feeling inferior. A baby doesn't feel inferior to an adult but simply realizes it's a baby and needs help from adults. God works with each person at the stage of growth they are in. God gives grace where He sees a person with a willing heart who wants to grow.

If you have failed as a Christian and have had the devil steal from you, you can be restored. Joel 2:25 says that God will restore to you the years that the locust, cankerworm, caterpillar and palmerworm have eaten. Those insects represent the devil stealing from a person's life. When they attack a plant, one eats the root, one eats the stem, one eats the leaf and the other one eats the fruit. The plant is totally destroyed after these four insects are finished.

Jesus said in John 10:10 that the thief (the devil) comes to steal, kill and destroy, but He has come to give us life and life more abundant. The Lord restores whatever has been destroyed if we turn to Him, turn from sin and believe His Word. He can rebuild the foundations of our lives as we yield to Him and in faith act upon His Word. He'll help you to bear fruit again and become effective for the Kingdom of God.

CHAPTER 5
LOVE

But the fruit of the Spirit is love....

Galatians 5:22

As we examine the fruit of the Spirit, we see that the first fruit mentioned is what the entire law and scriptures are based upon: *Love!* In fact, Jesus said in Mark 12:30 if we love God with all our heart, soul, mind and strength, and love our neighbor as we love ourselves, we'll keep all of God's Word.

All of the fruit of the Spirit are contained in love. Like an orange with many segments, love has segments such as patience, humility, faithfulness, etc. If we walk in love, we'll walk in all the other eight fruit of the Spirit. **"For all the law is fulfilled in one word, even in this; Thou shalt love thy neighbour as thyself"** (Galatians 5:14).

The word *love* is excessively overused in our society, expressing an attitude about anything from people to foods to clothes to pets or other things. For example, a person might say, "I love my husband (or wife)," and later on say, "I love football," or "I love ice cream." Fortunately, the Greeks are more specific in their definition and use of the word *love*. The three Greek words that describe *love* which we will discuss are *agape*, *phileo*, and *eros*.

When you are born again, you receive the God-kind of love – *agape* – into your heart. It is unselfish and unconditional. It is not based upon whether or not the person receiving love reciprocates.

In common terms, it is not a "because of" love. For example, "I love you *because* you make me feel good." What if the person doesn't always make you feel good? Does love stop at this point? *Agape* love continues to love "in spite of." This is how Jesus loves us.

Vine's Expository Dictionary relates it this way: "Christian (*agape*) love has God for its primary object, and expresses itself first of all in implicit obedience to His commandments. If we truly love God, we'll love the way He tells us to love. This love *is not an impulse from the feelings. It does not always run with the natural inclinations, nor does it spend itself only upon those for whom some affinity is discovered.*"[46] It is a selfless love, willing to deny itself for the benefit of the other person. This love will go so far as dying for its enemies. **"But God commendeth his love toward us, in that, while we were yet sinners, Christ died for us"** (Romans 5:8). Jesus actually introduced *agape* love into society.

Agape love is based upon a quality decision, a deliberate choice—not on a feeling. Just as Jesus chose to love people in spite of the fact that they nailed Him to a cross and crucified Him, we must choose to love people around our lives in spite of their actions toward us. *Agape* love is a choice we make on a daily basis.

We may not "feel" love at times when we choose to love some people. Jesus didn't feel a warm "mushy gushy" feeling when He hung on the cross. He felt pain and agony and He suffered, but He chose to love us and lay down His life for all mankind as a sacrifice for our sins. However, look at the harvest of lives that have been changed and have held true to Him to this day. He is receiving the fruit of the seed of His life which He sowed. Ephesians 5:2 says to us as Christians, **"And walk in love, as Christ also hath loved us, and hath given himself for us an offering and a sacrifice to God for a sweetsmelling savour."**

Some Christians have never experienced walking in *deliberate love* toward those who don't deserve it or toward those who have treated them wrongly. This is why the world has yet to be won to Jesus Christ. His love within us and through us is the witness that we are "Jesus people." John 13:35 says, **"By this shall all men know that ye are my disciples, if ye have love one to another."** Many who bear the label of "Christian" need to check their "love life."

Salvation Is Based Upon Love

Another important truth that every Christian must realize is that our salvation and eternity in heaven are based upon our love walk. First John 3:14-16 says:

We know that we have passed from death unto life, because we love the brethren. He that loveth not his brother abideth in death.

Whosoever hateth his brother is a murderer: and ye know that no murderer hath eternal life abiding in him.

Hereby perceive we the love of God, because he laid down his life for us: and we ought to lay down our lives for the brethren.

You know whether or not you are born again and have God in you by the fact that you love others (1 John 4:7,8).

Those Who Walk in Love
Have Clearer Direction

If you feel like you have been "stumbling around" in your life and it has been hard to find the right direction, check your "love life."

He that loveth his brother abideth in the light, and there is none occasion of stumbling in him.

But he that hateth his brother is in darkness, and walketh in darkness, and knoweth not whither he goeth, because that darkness hath blinded his eyes.

1 John 2:10,11

35

Love Beyond Feelings

Love that is based upon choice is not easy for your feelings. Jesus chose to love us in spite of how people treated Him, and He loved before we loved Him in return. We do have the ability to love by choice in spite of how we feel, because Romans 5:5 says that **"the love of God is shed abroad in our hearts by the Holy Ghost."** You have the love of God once you receive Jesus as Lord and Savior. He is love.

I heard Corrie ten Boom's testimony of how she was speaking at a Christian meeting and a man came up to her to shake her hand. Immediately she recognized him as a former concentration camp guard who had been instrumental in the death of her sister. She said at first she felt bitter anger, but then out of her heart and mouth came words of love and forgiveness. She said it amazed her, and she remembered the scripture in Romans 5:5. She knew then she was free of the bitterness and that God's love had taken control of her life. Jesus actually gives us grace to love others beyond human ability and in this there is freedom. The more you choose to love with *agape* love, the more it becomes a natural impulse in your life.

Love Will Grow

As we said earlier, the fruit of the Spirit are like muscles in our bodies that have to be developed and grow. We choose to walk in each fruit and each time we do, that spiritual muscle is exercised and grows a little stronger. The more you choose to love, the more loving you will become and the more you will look like Jesus to the people around your life.

Eros Love

The next Greek word for love which we will discuss is *eros*.

The world seems to be most familiar with *eros* love, which refers to physical love, and is governed by the five senses—what we see, hear, taste, touch and smell.

Many relationships start out on the *eros* level (physical love) when a man and woman are physically attracted to each other. God is left out. In their attempt to grow closer to one another, eventually they end up in sin. Ultimately, the *eros* relationship will break up. This is because *eros* love, apart from God, is based upon gratifying self, so when self becomes tired of that person and is not fulfilled, it ends.

If *eros* is placed in the proper position, it is good. This is because God placed the five senses within us so we can find fulfillment in the marriage relationship as long as *agape* love is the foundation of the relationship.

Phileo Love

The third word used for love in the Greek language is *phileo*. *Phileo* describes brotherly love or human love. There is a city in the United States known as "Philadelphia." It was named the city of brotherly love. The name is derived from this word, *phileo*.

This kind of love can be very strong and tender. Some people have operated in this kind of love without even knowing God and have given their lives for others because of it. You probably have heard of people who, during times of war or crisis, have given their lives for others or for their country. But *phileo* love is also based on feelings. When one is operating solely in *phileo* love, he gives his love to a person he has some feeling or affinity for.

Relationships built solely upon *phileo* or human love often are terminated when arguments arise, or the feeling of having some things in common changes, or the "buzz" is gone from the relationship. Sometimes in marriage this stormy type of relationship survives long enough to bring a form of religion into the picture, but such a relationship often ends in divorce because the foundation of human love is not solid. In order for a marriage relationship to last and be filled with joy and peace, you must have *agape* love as the core of it. Love based upon feelings cannot last because human feelings can change with circumstances.

Phileo, however, is needed in a relationship. When a couple begins a relationship based on *agape*, then moves toward establishing a strong friendship, the marriage will have the strength to succeed and last.

Agape Love

When a couple starts their relationship with *agape*, the God-kind of love—unselfish love—they will be willing to give up their own selfish desires for the benefit of the other person. They will keep their physical responses under control, because love is patient and willing to wait until the appointed time of marriage. Later on in marriage, they know they can trust each other because they kept themselves and conquered their desires before they married. When *agape* is the foundation, they will grow together through the years as best friends rather than grow apart.

Agape love has self-control. *Eros* love says, "I can't wait until marriage." *Agape* love says, "I choose to wait until marriage." *Agape* love allows time so that both people get to know each other and can enter into a relationship where both have chosen to love each other "in spite of" and not "because of" what the other person can do for them.

Agape love is God's highest and most fulfilling plan for every person, whether in a marriage relationship or in our daily relationships with all people. As we choose to love unconditionally, we will overcome offenses and be able to grow stronger in love no matter what tests we may face.

God's plan is that *agape* always be in control of your life, leading and directing you, spilling over into every area of your life.

The best definition the Bible gives us for *agape* love is found in 1 Corinthians 13:4-8 AMP:

Love endures long and is patient and kind; love never is envious nor boils over with jealousy, is not boastful or vainglorious, does not display itself haughtily.

It is not conceited (arrogant and inflated with pride); it is not rude (unmannerly) and does not act unbecomingly. Love (God's love in us) does not insist on its own rights or its own way, for it is not self-seeking; it is not touchy or fretful or resentful; it takes no account of the evil done to it [it pays no attention to a suffered wrong].

It does not rejoice at injustice and unrighteousness, but rejoices when right and truth prevail.

Love bears up under anything and everything that comes, is ever ready to believe the best of every person, its hopes are fadeless under all circumstances, and it endures everything [without weakening].

Love never fails [never fades out or becomes obsolete or comes to an end]....

Love Is Patient

"Now the God of patience and consolation grant you to be likeminded one toward another according to Christ Jesus" (Romans 15:5). Part of possessing the "mind of Christ" is possessing the quality of patience.

If we are to become likeminded as Jesus and walk "in Him," then we must seek to develop in patience as He is patient. God, in His mercy, has lovingly forgiven, endured and given people many opportunities to make changes and turn to Him. In spite of people's stubbornness, He loves and readily receives them when they repent and turn to Him.

As we've pastored over the years, I've found that working with people will either develop patience or cause them to close themselves off from those who wear on their nerves or rub them the wrong way. We choose continually if we will let His fruit grow or die in our lives. People from all walks of life come around us. Some need time to observe and experience *agape* love before they change. Patient love can bring others into growing beyond those habits or personalities that previously provoked you.

I've watched people walk out of abusive behavior, alcoholism, drug addiction, immorality, critical attitudes, unforgiveness, stubbornness, pride and self-centeredness and become so free that they are now willing to reach out to help others.

How many marriages could last and grow strong if marriage partners would develop patience with one another? My husband and I realized that it would take a joint effort to have a good marriage relationship. We were two distinct individuals having two separate minds and two different personalities and backgrounds which had to be melted and molded into one.

I was a very outgoing and outspoken person who enjoyed talking a lot while Billy Joe was more conservative, although he was also outgoing and friendly. I would barely get to appointments on time, while he was always early and on time. Rather than get into strife, we decided to communicate with each other how to better plan and meet our schedules. We also realized that having a second car could benefit our relationship. He has smiled and loved me many times in the midst of my talking. I have adjusted my ways, but I'm thankful for his love when I forget and talk more than necessary. Over the years we've prayed for each other. Billy Joe has had to be very patient with me at times when I've fallen short of his expectations, and he says I've been patient with him. Years ago we both made a decision to cover one another when one fell behind in some way, and to help each other.

Above all things have intense and unfailing love for one another, for love covers a multitude of sins [forgives and disregards the offenses of others].

1 Peter 4:8 AMP

Every person has times when they need the mercy and help of

someone else. What we sow towards others we will reap. If you want people to be patient and understanding with you, then be patient and understanding with others. If you become a critical, strife-filled person, no one will want to be around you. Jesus people will attract other people to their lives through the "sweet fruit" flowing through them.

We in the Body of Christ must make every effort to walk in patience and love to cover one another's faults. Praying in the Spirit at these times will help us overcome. I have found that praying in the Spirit can calm my emotions, open my mind up to solutions and answers that I need, and give me God's direction and grace to do whatever He says.

Love Is Kind

Ephesians 4:32 AMP says:

And become useful and helpful and kind to one another, tenderhearted (compassionate, understanding, loving-hearted)....

Kindness is a quality that has almost been neglected in our generation because of the popular self-seeking attitudes which exist in society. Fast-paced living has subtly caused
people to barely have time for themselves, much less for others. Some people feel that if they take time to be kind to others, something will be neglected that can benefit themselves.

The Word of God looks at people and situations quite differently. **"Let each of you esteem and look upon and be concerned for not [merely] his own interests, but also each for the interests of others"** (Philippians 2:4 AMP).

Love sees others' needs and steps out to fill them, no matter who it is. In Luke 10:30-37, Jesus told the parable of the Good Samaritan. In this story, the Good Samaritan performed a kindness to one who had been considered an enemy. This is a perfect illustration of one who saw a need and took time to step out to fulfill it because of the compassion of God within him.

The Good Samaritan didn't have to be kind. He was actually of

41

another race than the man in need. [As the older saints of God used to say, "Hear me now."] The man in need represented a race of people who felt superior to the Samaritans and wouldn't associate with them. The Samaritan had to forget racism to demonstrate kindness. He also had to forget about the time it was taking him and about what others might think about him helping the man of another race.

As you exercise your spiritual muscles of godliness, add brotherly kindness to it (2 Peter 1:7). God's kindness is exemplified in our actions and not just in our words. **"...faith without works is dead..."** (James 2:26).

Love Is Not Envious

The God-kind of love is excited over the blessings of others. *Agape* love isn't upset (resentful) at others being blessed.

Proverbs 14:30 says, **"A sound heart is the life of the flesh: but envy the rottenness of the bones."** Envy can actually cause your body to become weak and sick. James 3:16 says, **"For where envying and strife is, there is confusion and every evil work."** Envy and strife open the door to the devil to bring all kinds of evil against the one who has envy or strife. It isn't worth it to hold envy and strife in your heart. Job 5:2 says envy can actually kill a person who allows it in his or her life.

Keep a healthy, positive attitude toward others. For as you continue to seek first the things of the Kingdom of God, He will add "all these things" *unto* your life (Matthew 6:33), and when He adds to your life, there will be no sorrow with it (Proverbs 10:22).

Love Is Not Boastful, Vainglorious, Puffed Up, or Conceited

> **For [it is] not [the man] who praises and commends himself who is approved and accepted, but [it is the person] whom the Lord accredits and commends.**
>
> **2 Corinthians 10:18** AMP

When I was a student at Oral Roberts University, one professor shared Proverbs 18:16 with our class: *"If you are gifted and talented, your gift will make room for you."* Years later I heard a speaker quote this same scripture verse from another perspective: *"The giving of your gift will make room for you and bring you before great men."* The more you give your gift to serve the Lord with no desire for personal gain, God will promote you.

You need to be willing to be used of the Lord in small settings and be faithful to give your gift whenever it is needed. There's a balance of availing yourself and being pushy. A "pushy" attitude indicates pride and a lack of godly humility and dependence on God. Also, human nature prompts us to emphasize the fact that "I" prophesy or "I" cast out devils. Or "I" sang and people gave a standing ovation. Your emphasis should not be on the personal "I," but let God be the One Who is magnified.

James 4:6 AMP says, **"But He gives us more and more grace (power of the Holy Spirit, to meet this evil tendency and all others fully). That is why He says, *God sets Himself against the proud and haughty*, but gives grace [continually] to the lowly (those who are humble enough to receive it)."** *Grace* means "divine favor." God will give favor to the humble.

"Therefore humble yourselves [demote, lower yourselves in your own estimation] under the mighty hand of God, that in due time He may exalt you" (1 Peter 5:6 AMP). There is a "due season" for your exaltation, but let it come from the Lord.

I grew up in small towns, and I had many opportunities to sing. I guess you could say that I was "a big fish in little ponds." But when I went to Oral Roberts University, there were many other talented people there. God kept my singing opportunities to a minimum, because He wanted to teach me some more important lessons. God was doing an inner work on my attitude during this time to grow His character in me. (Many times back then I felt like Moses in the days of his preparation on the back side of the desert before God really used him.) I wanted to be used so much and do great things for God, but I was being tempered.

When my husband and I were led into an evangelistic ministry and later into a pastorate, God began using the gift He had given me to a much greater degree. He has taught me, however, that I am *totally* dependent upon Him. No matter how talented or trained a person is, if there is no anointing, nothing will happen. We must have God's divine flow and that comes only as we are dependent upon Him and seeking Him daily.

Humility is a *total* dependence upon God. Thinking and speaking in a degrading manner about yourself is not humility; it is actually a form of self-exaltation. Don't get caught in that trap! Humility is realizing everything you have and are is because of Jesus. It is realizing you need to draw on Him daily.

Humble yourself unto God and let Him exalt you in His time!

Love Doesn't Behave Unbecomingly

In our society today, most people with wrong behavior want to blame someone or something for it. Usually it is blamed on the fact that they were from a dysfunctional family, or they had difficult circumstances. They continue wrong behavior and attitude problems, feeling justified. God doesn't let us use Him to excuse our lack of conscience. Growth demands that we accept responsibility for our actions and attitudes and bring them into submission to the lordship of Jesus.

Always attempt to be mannerly and gracious with whomever you're with. Remember to consider the feelings of others. Be sensitive to the offenses that may cause others difficulty. Love motivates us to be sensitive to the setting we find ourselves in and helps us to know what is fitting.

Ecclesiastes 3:1 AMP says, **"To everything there is a season, and a time for every matter or purpose under heaven."** God will help you if you listen to Him to know what is appropriate. You'll be led by His Spirit in your behavior.

Ecclesiastes says there's a time to laugh and a time to cry; there's a time to be silent and a time to speak; there's a time to mourn and a time to dance.

As you listen within your spirit, God will be your guide in every situation to act becomingly.

Love Doesn't Insist Upon Having Its Own Way

Do you seek to do what will benefit you or what will benefit others?

In John 5:30 AMP Jesus said:

> **I am able to do nothing from Myself [independently, of My own accord—but only as I am taught by God and as I get His orders]. Even as I hear, I judge [I decide as I am bidden to decide. As the voice comes to Me, so I give a decision], and My judgment is right (just, righteous),** *because I do not seek or consult My own will* **[I have no desire to do what is pleasing to Myself, My own aim, My own purpose]** *but only the will and pleasure of the Father Who sent Me.*

Jesus sought to do God's will even if it hurt, and He didn't insist on His own way. Love seeks God's will, not self-will; and Jesus Christ is the perfect example of selflessness for man to follow. In the Garden of Gethsemane Jesus **"...threw Himself upon the ground on His face and prayed saying, My Father, if it is possible, let this cup pass away from Me; nevertheless, not what I will [not what I desire],** *but as You will and desire"* (Matthew 26:39 AMP).

Jesus did not want to go through the cross experience, but He knew that the salvation of mankind depended upon Him carrying out God's plan. Jesus exemplified total selflessness, and in so doing, God gave Him a name which is above all names—in heaven, on earth, and under the earth.

It is in self-denial and giving to others that we keep an open channel for the divine flow of God's love to move through us, as is seen in Luke 9:23: **"And to all he said, 'If anyone wishes to be a follower of mine,** *he must leave self behind; day after day* **he must take up his cross, and come with me'"** (*The New English Bible*).

Love Is Not Touchy, Resentful, or Easily Provoked

God has provided a way for you to stay in His love walk when people seem to rub you the wrong way. God's way to remain in love is similar to the old cliché—"Just let things roll off of you like water off a duck's back."

Ducks have small oil beads under their feathers. When they are going to move out in water, they will sit on the bank of the water's edge and pick their feathers. The oily substance from underneath the feathers saturates them so that when they move out upon the water, they won't sink. The oily substance stops the water from soaking into their back. Thus, they are able to float on the water.

God wants to anoint us with the oil of His Spirit through time spent with Him so that as we go about our day, offenses will not sink us but we will stay afloat.

When people say things that would normally hurt or offend you, you can let it roll off of you like water off a duck's back! **"Great peace have they which *love thy law* [the Word of God]: and nothing shall offend them"** (Psalm 119:165). If you set your heart and mind to think on things which are true, pure, honest, lovely, just, and of good report (Philippians 4:8), you will be more conscious of God's Word than of your own personal feelings. It is much more important to walk in the freedom and peace of God than to carry "a chip on your shoulders." If you allow yourself to be easily angered, then others are controlling your life. Get control of your emotions and you'll get control of your life.

Always remember that you can do all things *through Christ* Who strengthens you (Philippians 4:13). His grace is sufficient to help you forgive, release offenses and go forward (2 Corinthians 12:7-10).

Love Doesn't Keep a List of Wrongs

Do not keep a list of wrongdoings, whether it be in a marriage relationship or in a friendship relationship. The God-kind of love *forgives* and *forgets* offenses. There should be no secretly kept, running list to pull out and use as ammunition against another person. Bringing up past grievances only heightens the wall between people, regardless of the type of relationship involved.

When you forgive anyone, I do too . . . A further reason for forgiveness is to keep from being outsmarted by Satan; for we know what he is trying to do.

2 Corinthians 2:10,11 TLB

Instant forgiveness will close the door to Satan and his schemes in your life. You cannot afford to keep a list of wrongs! Let go of them, and let God help you to walk in peace with others as far as it lies within you (Romans 12:18).

Jesus said in Mark 11:25,26:

And when ye stand praying, forgive, if ye have ought against any: that your Father also which is in heaven may forgive you your trespasses.

But if ye do not forgive, neither will your Father which is in heaven forgive your trespasses.

Ought is anything whatever, to any degree. It could be the smallest amount. If unforgiveness toward another still lingers in the smallest amount, your own trespasses cannot be forgiven by God. That means you cannot be saved if you cannot forgive because God cannot forgive you. This is serious.

How do you forgive when you've been extremely hurt? You forgive in obedience to God's Word with your faith. Everything in God's Word is by faith, not feelings. By faith you begin to say, "I forgive and I receive God's forgiveness in my life." By faith you begin to pray for those who've done wrong that God's Spirit would be released to work in their lives. Feelings will ultimately change as you speak and act in faith. Sometimes God will have people do an act of kindness toward the very person or persons who have hurt them. This seals the forgiveness.

You may be asking, "How can this happen?" By the supernatural grace of God coming upon a person's life. Jesus did it on the cross when He cried, **"Father, forgive them; for they know not what they do"** (Luke 23:34). Did they know? They knew they were whipping Him, cursing and spitting on Him and crucifying Him. What did He mean? He meant they didn't realize that they were being manipulated by demonic powers to kill the One Who loved them most. Nor did they realize it was all in God's plan to redeem mankind back to God who would believe in Him.

Release offense and let God handle these people. Either they will come to repentance, or go through His judgment. The important thing is for *you* to be free from all ill will and walk in God's blessings and salvation.

Love Does Not Rejoice at Injustice, Is Not Happy When Evil Befalls Another, Does Not Rejoice Over Misfortunes of Others

When a person has been caught in a fault, rather than tell them, "I told you so," or feel disgusted with them, go to them if possible and talk with them. You can pray for them and believe for God to work a miracle (Galatians 6:1). Love confronts when wrong has been done, but it also gives help to overcome.

If you love someone you will be loyal to him no matter what the cost. You will always believe in him, always expect the best of him, and always stand your ground in defending him.

1 Corinthians 13:7 TLB

When you pray for someone with the love of God, you will release your faith for them. You'll believe that God can raise them up out of difficult circumstances. You will stand with them against Satan's accusations.

The Love of God Never Gives Up on People

Jesus' love never gave up on the disciples, no matter how often they failed. John, the author of the three epistles on love, was the disciple Jesus called "the son of thunder," because he and his brother wanted to call fire down from heaven to consume the Samaritan village which did not receive Jesus. Later, John was to be called "the disciple of love." The Spirit of Christ transformed John's life, and it will also transform your life.

God's love never comes to an end. If you feel you are at the end of the rope in your faith for someone, don't give up. God's love will cause you to triumph in your stand. The love of God is the foundation for faith, because faith works by love (Galatians 5:6). God's love is our source of living.

Walking in love encompasses all of the fruit of the Spirit, and walking in love is walking in the Spirit!

Aids To Walking in Love

Some dynamic aids that will help you walk in love are:

1. Decide to love. Love is a decision, not a feeling.

2.Watch your mouth. **"Let no corrupt communication proceed out of your mouth, but that which is good to the use of edifying, that it may minister grace unto the hearers. And grieve not the Holy Spirit of God, whereby ye are sealed unto the day of redemption. Let all bitterness, and wrath, and anger, and clamour, and evil speaking, be put away from you, with all malice: And be ye kind one to another, tenderhearted, forgiving one another, even as God for Christ's sake hath forgiven you"** (Ephesians 4:29-32).

3. Be the first to admit that you are wrong, and ask forgiveness no matter who is at fault.

4. Develop an openness with people. Endeavor to communicate in an honest, open way.

5. Pray in the Spirit. **"But you, beloved, build yourselves up [founded] on your most holy faith [make progress, rise like an edifice higher and higher],** *praying in the Holy Spirit;* **guard and** *keep yourselves in the love of God;* **expect and patiently wait for the mercy of our Lord Jesus Christ (the Messiah) - [which will bring you] unto life eternal"** (Jude 20,21 AMP).

6. Spend time *daily* in God's Word. **"But he who keeps (treasures) His Word [who bears in mind His precepts, who observes His message in its entirety], truly in him has the love of and for God been perfected (completed, reached maturity). By this we may perceive (know, recognize, and be sure) that**

we are in Him" (1 John 2:5 AMP).

    7. Use your faith to believe that God's Word will be perfected in your life and that He will work through you to bring His love into the lives of others around you.

Endotes

[46]Vine, p. 693.

CHAPTER 6
JOY

But the fruit of the Spirit is . . . joy

Galatians 5:22

W hen you are born again and you experience God's conversion in your life, there is a joy that comes within you resulting from being right with God and forgiven of sin. The Bible says the Kingdom of God comes into your life. That Kingdom **"...is not meat and drink; but righteousness, and peace, and joy in the Holy Ghost"** (Romans 14:17).

This scripture simply means that the Kingdom of God does not consist of rules and regulations, do's and don'ts, but is a relationship of right standing with God, producing peace and joy in the Holy Spirit. Out of that relationship of right standing, you want to do right because you want to please Him. When you truly love someone, you don't want to lose the good relationship that you have with them, so you avoid anything that would hurt the relationship.

The greatest joy you can experience in this life is that of accepting Jesus Christ as your Lord and Savior. However, as any Christian knows, that feeling of joy can change if a person does not continue fellowshipping daily with God in prayer and in the Word. This is because the world around us creates circumstances to stop that flow of joy. You see, the Word of God is our stabilizing key to walk in continual victory and triumph.

God's Word shows us that our victory or triumph and the reason to rejoice is not because we always *feel* happy but because

Jesus defeated Satan's dominion over our lives and set us free to live in His newness of life (John 8:31,32). Jesus' victory is our victory (2 Corinthians 2:14). Satan cannot defeat you or hold you once you begin to know the truth of your freedom. Jesus freed you from sin, compulsive behavior patterns, dysfunctional lifestyles, sickness and disease, depression, grief, mental torment, fear, confusion, bitterness and everything else under the curse of the law (Galatians 3:13,14,29; Deuteronomy 28).

Once you know your redemption, then you choose to walk in it. If you haven't already discovered it, you will discover that you *choose* to rejoice just as you *choose* to love or to walk in any of the other fruit of the Spirit. Remember, your will is very strong. Your will determines or chooses your actions and reactions all the time. There will be times when you *feel* joyful, but other times when you don't. This is why you must decide that you are going to "live by faith" in God's Word and not by your feelings.

Your faith to act upon God's Word will allow the opportunity for your feelings to follow. Your feelings will actually begin to experience what your faith begins to act upon. Allow me to explain. Years ago when my husband and I began Victory Christian Center, we had taken a loan from a bank to have a building for the church to meet in. The church grew quickly to over 2,000 people, but we were just surviving financially. The interest rate at that time was floating and tied to the prime interest rate which went as high as 15 percent. The building note was $3.3 million. At one point in the beginning of the church, we sold our only car to pay a ministry bill. God provided us a car to drive for several months free of charge without us even telling anyone our situation.

In two years we reduced the note to $3.1 million, but it was very difficult. During this time we had to reduce our staff and help them locate jobs elsewhere. We outgrew the location in a short time but were locked into a financial burden and seeming limitation. We even attempted, through man's reasoning, to purchase a port-a-mod structure. Since this was not God's direction, we sold it.

On a personal side, we were walking through months of

standing in faith for the healing of our daughter which most people were unaware of. During this time we also received a couple of negative prophecies from people who prophesied out of their own minds. Those prophecies did not happen. There were other situations with people around our lives that we chose to walk in love toward.

In the midst of this, one day in my time with God I asked Him to have someone call and encourage me. Immediately in my spirit I heard the words, **"David encouraged himself in the Lord his God"** (1 Samuel 30:6). I didn't want to hear that. I said to God, "I have scriptural basis to cry: Psalm 3:4—**'I cried unto the Lord with my voice, and he heard me out of his holy hill.'"** Then in my spirit I heard these words, "Rejoice in the Lord and begin to sing, 'The Joy of the Lord Is My Strength.'" Again, these were scriptures brought to my memory (Nehemiah 8:10; Philippians 4:4). Then I heard Him say inside of my heart, "Get up and dance while you sing" (Psalm 150:4). I did not feel like it at all! I did it, however, out of obedience, crying as I sang.

Suddenly, the burden of it all lifted and I began to feel joyful. I felt freedom and I knew inside of me that we were going to make it and things were going to turn. It took a process of two years before we saw everything turn, but it began that day for me in my spirit.

The sweet thing that God did for me that day after I encouraged myself was to have two or three other people call to encourage me, whom I had not heard from in a long time. Even if they had not called, I had already moved into the joy of His victory.

Romans 4:20,21 says that Abraham **"staggered not at the promise of God through unbelief; but was strong in faith, *giving glory to God*; and being fully persuaded, that what he had promised, he was able also to perform."**

In order to be strong in faith, we must learn to enter into the joy of the Lord. This requires us to praise and worship the Lord before we see any change in our circumstances. It is a choice we make to praise and worship and glorify God.

The psalmist said:

I *will* bless the Lord at all times: his praise shall continually be in my mouth.

Psalm 34:1

I *will* sing praises unto my God while I have any being.

Psalm 146:2

This is the day which the Lord hath made; we *will* rejoice and be glad in it.

Psalm 118:24

Throughout the Psalms, we see that over and over again, praising God and rejoicing were *acts of the will*.

In the New Testament, when you read about the trials and the persecution that Paul faced, you will notice he also understood the strength and victory in rejoicing and praising God. Acts 16:25 tells the incident of Paul and Silas in prison. At midnight they prayed and began singing praises to God loud enough that the prisoners heard them. Notice, in their horrible situation they didn't start blaming one another and complaining. Instead, they focused their attention on the Lord.

In any test or difficult time, if we can focus our hearts and minds on prayer and praise, God will break through for us. Praise stills the enemy and brings strength to our lives. Psalm 8:2 says, **"Out of the mouth of babes and sucklings hast thou *ordained strength* because of thine enemies, that thou mightest still the enemy and the avenger."** Jesus quoted this verse in Matthew 21:16 and inserted the word *praise* in it, saying, **"Out of the mouth of babes and sucklings thou hast *perfected praise.*"**

The word *ordained* in the Hebrew (*yasad*) means to lay a foundation.[47] Through praise, God lays a foundation of strength in our lives to overcome whatever situation we face and through praise we "still" (stop) the enemy and the avenger (the devil and his demonic powers).

When the prisoners heard Paul and Silas rejoicing, they were awestruck at what they heard. The prison doors opened supernaturally and everyone's bands were loosed (Acts 16:25,26).

Praising the Lord will bring immediate results:

1. Praise gets your mind off of you and onto the Lord.

2. Praise will shake the circumstances.

3. Praising and rejoicing in the Lord will open prison doors which have been locked in your life.

4. Praising and rejoicing in the Lord will loosen the bands of the devil from you and from those around you.

5. Praise brings the supernatural manifestation of God on the scene, which can lead sinners to salvation.

Joy Produces Strength

Praise releases the joy of the Lord in our lives, and the joy of the Lord is our strength (Nehemiah 8:10). If we let go of our joy, we let go of our strength. If we cease praising God or we choose to not praise Him or rejoice, we choose to let go of our joy and strength to overcome. This is how some Christians' spiritual foundation becomes shaken or destroyed, because they have chosen not to receive the strength of the Lord that He has provided.

God has provided everything we need to live, through His promises, but we must choose to act upon those promises to possess them in our lives. First Thessalonians 5:18 says, **"In every thing give thanks: for this is the will of God in Christ Jesus concerning you."** God's will is for us to praise and give thanks to Him *in* the midst of whatever circumstance we may be in. He doesn't mean for us to thank Him *for* everything that happens, but to thank Him *in the midst of* everything that happens.

We thank Him that He is still Lord and His Word is still true. We thank Him for Who He is and for what He has done. Ephesians 5:20 has been said by one book author to mean that we are to thank God for everything that happens, even accidents, sickness, the death of loved ones, people living in sin, etc. This scripture does not mean we should thank God for the destructive works of the devil, but that we should thank God for all things that are attributed unto God. John 10:10 says that it is the thief (the devil) who comes to steal, kill and destroy, but Jesus has come to give life and life more abundantly.

Jesus is the expressed will of God (our Father). John 14:9 says, **"...he that hath seen me hath seen the Father."** Jesus did not cause sickness or accidents. He did not go around killing people. He healed, He saved and He forgave people. He brought life and did good to people wherever He went (Acts 10:38).

God is good and the devil is evil. We do not thank God for things that the devil has done, but we thank Him that in the midst of bad things, Jesus can turn it, take our lives forward and restore us.

Those who choose to rejoice and praise God whether circumstances are good or bad will go forward in life and overcome whatever they face. How could Paul write such a letter of encouragement and joy from prison when he wrote to the Philippians to rejoice? He had found that his source of joy was in his relationship with Jesus Christ and that doesn't change with circumstances (see Philippians 3:1; 4:4). What does it mean to rejoice? The prefix "*re-*" indicates to do it over again. We choose to *re-joy* and renew our strength in the Lord on a daily basis.

No One Can Take Your Joy

John 16:22 says that no man can take your joy from you. That means the only way we lose our joy is if we let it go. As we read the Scripture, we can see all that Paul and others went through did not control their joy in the Lord (2 Corinthians 4:8-11, 16-18). I believe it was because, "[They looked] **not at the things which are seen, but at the things which are not seen: for the things which are seen are temporal; but the things which are not seen are eternal"** (2 Corinthians 4:18).

What is Paul saying? He had come to the revelation of the fact that as long as he kept his thoughts and attention on the Word of God (the eternal), the things which he could see with his natural eyes would change eventually. The word *temporal* in 2 Corinthians 4:18 means lasting only for a time; of or limited by time; transitory. The Greek word for *temporal* is *proskairos* and means "for a season."[48] One minister has said that it means "subject to change." The word *eternal* means forever the same; always true or valid; unchanging.[49]

Everything we see with our natural eyes is temporal. It is subject to change and of a limited time. However, God's Word does not change. (In Matthew 24:35, the Greek for *pass* is *parerchomai*, meaning to perish. Heaven and earth will perish, but His *words* will remain unchanged forever.)[50] Our joy is in God's Word that does not change, even though circumstances may change. But we can actually change circumstances if we believe and keep our focus on the Word of God.

James 1:2 says, **"My brethren, count it all joy when ye fall into divers temptations."** The Greek word for *fall* is *peripipto*, which means to be caught by.[51] The Greek word for *divers temptations* is *peirasmos*, which means trials or an attack.[52] It is a trial of *any kind*, not necessarily a temptation to sin. So we could read this verse as, *"Brethren, count it all joy when you are caught by any trial or attack where you are tested to see how you are going to handle it."*

Verse 3 goes on to say, **"Knowing this, that the trying of your faith worketh patience."**

Verses 2-4 in *The Amplified Version* say:

Consider it wholly joyful, my brethren, whenever you are enveloped in or encounter trials of any sort or fall into various temptations.

Be assured and understand that the trial and proving of your faith bring out endurance and steadfastness and patience.

But let endurance and steadfastness and patience have full play and do a thorough work, so that you may be [people] perfectly and fully developed [with no defects], lacking in nothing.

Notice, the test itself doesn't work patience in you but when you choose to rejoice in the Lord and release your faith in His Word, patience can work in you the ability to overcome. Patience then develops maturity in your life so that at the end of the trial you do not lack anything you've believed for.

The world around us only knows joy in circumstances that are happy. Since this is not reality, many people in the world who do not know Jesus in a personal, living relationship, seek temporary joy in relationships with people, alcohol, drugs, job success, educational achievements, vacations, entertainment, etc. The momentary buzz of joy they feel numbs the bad circumstances, but then reality comes back.

Ecclesiastes 7:6 NAS says, **"For as the crackling of thorn bushes under a pot, so is the laughter of the fool, and this too is futility."** Thorn bushes were used as fuel for fire because they burn so quickly. Worldly joy is like thorn bushes. It goes as quickly as it comes.

There is a lasting joy that remains within a person when Jesus becomes their Lord and His Word becomes final authority in their life.

My husband told me that during Christmas holidays when he was a little boy, the glitter of the tinsel and the opening of gifts were so exciting and he felt such joy. But he said that when the holidays came to a close, he felt such emptiness, such a letdown. What an accurate description of worldly joy. It never quite measures up to your expectations.

Some people pretend to be happy by wearing a smile on their face every time they go out in public, but as you begin to talk with them, you realize they are hiding behind the smile. I believe Christians should smile regardless of the situations they are in. In fact, Proverbs 15:13 says, **"A merry heart maketh a cheerful countenance."**

The joy of the Lord will show on your face. It goes down deep within the soul and is a result of fellowship with Jesus. It isn't based on whether you laugh all the time. Laughter is only one part of it. The joy of the Lord can be expressed through praising God, testifying, singing, clapping, laughing, or just smiling.

There are some Christians, however, who have not been walking in fellowship with Jesus and do not want others to think that they are not happy and strong on their own. These people often wear a mask of a smile so others will not ask questions. The Scripture speaks of this in Proverbs 14:13 TLB: **"Laughter cannot mask a heavy heart. When the laughter ends, the grief remains."** What causes a heavy heart? Many situations can cause heaviness:

1. *Sin* can cause a heaviness within. When you know that you've done something wrong and you feel badly about it, it robs that sense of freedom and innocence. Instead, there's guilt, shame and fear that someone will find out and it will hurt others. Some Christians have gone into depression over unrepented sin. The mercy of repentance is that it brings freedom from guilt, shame and fear. Faith in the cleansing blood of Jesus and forgiveness clears the slate in a person's life so they can go forward.

2. *Unforgiveness* causes heaviness of heart because bitterness held toward someone robs freedom within and the person holding the grudge forfeits their joy. They become so focused on being offended they can't see how they could release the person or persons to God. The fact is, their unforgiveness can't do anything but hurt themselves. They are afraid that if they forgive, the person will not have to pay for their hurt. Don't worry, God is able to handle other people. Why not release it to Him? Your own forgiveness from God and your salvation are at stake (Mark 11:25).

2. *Grief* over the loss of a loved one can cause heaviness of heart. The Bible says, **"...a broken spirit drieth the bones"** (Proverbs 17:22). It deteriorates a person's body physically.

When my husband's father went to heaven after a fatal accident over twenty-three years ago, Billy Joe and I shared a scripture with his mom from Isaiah 58:6-12. She made a decision to act upon God's Word in the midst of a time of grief and loss. She began visiting people in the hospital and nursing home after she got off work each day. Most of the people she visited, she had never met before, but she developed friendships with them. She also became involved in overseeing a women's ministry outreach. Years later she came to work with us in our ministry at Victory Christian Center. She has had the joy and peace of God through all of these years because she has given her life to bless others.

The principle of giving works. When we give to others, we are as blessed as they are. Giving people are more prone to be happy people. Self-centered or stingy people and those living in self-pity do not have the depth of joy in their lives. Usually other people do not enjoy being around them either.

Jesus said, **"It is more blessed to give than to receive"** (Acts 20:35). The giver rejoices more because it blesses him to see that the receiver is helped and encouraged by their giving. It brings a sense of fulfillment to the giver. That's why God is joyful. He's the greatest Giver of all!

Joy Brings Healing

"A happy heart is a good medicine and a cheerful mind works healing, but a broken spirit dries up the bones" (Proverbs 17:22 AMP).

Rejoicing in the Lord will actually loose the healing power of Jesus Christ to flow through your physical body. Medical science has documented records of people with terminal illnesses who rejoiced their way back to health! We have a reason to rejoice because of what Jesus has done and will do for us.

In Norman Cousins' book, *Anatomy of an Illness*, he wrote that his doctor found laughter reduced the inflammation and infection in his body. Through laughter he overcame an irreversible disease.

A 1990 Clemson University study showed that nursing home patients felt better after watching old comedies. These reports have led to hospitals adding laughter to their fight against illness. It was reported in "The Orange County Register," Tuesday, March

10, 1992, that a HUMOR project in Saratoga Springs, New York, awarded grants to twelve hospitals, nursing homes and other agencies to start humor programs.

Dr. Paul McGehee, a New Jersey psychologist who has researched laughter for over twenty years, said that one's frame of mind has an impact on the body's health system. Other studies show that after people laugh, they have more immunoglobulin A and other natural substances that fight off illness and kill pain. The heart rate increases. The oxygen supply to the brain is boosted and the blood flow improves. The body then relaxes and becomes calm. People sense their burdens are lifted. Does this sound like what the Bible has taught for years? Sometimes the world takes every other approach until it faces the fact that the Bible is true and it is relevant for every generation.

The Greek word for *joy* is *chara*, which means to be glad, to delight and rejoice; to be exuberant with joy and exultation.[53] Webster defines it, to be exuberant; to be full of life; uninhibited. He goes on to say it is showing exultation, which means to rejoice with jubilation and triumph.[54]

Scriptural Ways To Release Joy and Praise to God

Scriptural ways to release joy and praise to the Lord include:

1. *The song* - **"The Lord is my Strength and my [impenetrable] Shield; my heart trusts in, relies on, and confidently leans on Him, and I am helped; therefore my heart greatly rejoices, and with my song will I praise Him"** (Psalm 28:7 AMP).

The word *hallelujah* comes from the Hebrew word *Halal*, which means to be clear; to shine, to boast, to show, to rave, celebrate, to be clamorously foolish.[55] It can be spoken or sung.

Rejoice in the Lord, O ye righteous: for praise is comely [becoming, suitable, beautiful] **for the upright.**

Praise the Lord with harp: sing unto him with the psaltery and an instrument of ten strings.

Sing unto him a new song; play skilfully with a *loud noise.*

Psalm 33:1-3

2. *The shout* - "But let all those who take refuge and put their trust in You rejoice; let them ever sing and shout for joy, because You make a covering over them and defend them; let those also who love Your name be joyful in You and be in high spirits" (Psalm 5:11 AMP).

3. *Musical instruments* - "Let them praise His name in chorus and choir and with the [single or group] dance; let them sing praises to Him with the tambourine and lyre!" (Psalm 149:3 AMP). "Praise Him with tambourine and [single or group] dance; praise Him with stringed and wind instruments or flutes!" (Psalm 150:4 AMP).

4. *With the dance* - "Let them praise his name in the dance..." (Psalm 149:3). Second Samuel 6:14 says, "And David danced before the Lord with all his might" (Note: His wife Michal was embarrassed by her husband's rejoicing and freedom, and because she despised him in her heart, her womb was shut so that she could never bear children.)

5. *With the clapping of hands* - "O clap your hands, all you peoples! Shout to God with the voice of triumph and songs of joy!" (Psalm 47:1 AMP).

6. *With uplifted hands* - "So will I bless You while I live; I will lift up my hands in Your name" (Psalm 63:4 AMP).

7. *With laughter* - "When the Lord brought back the captives [who returned] to Zion, we were like those who dream [it seemed so unreal]. Then were our mouths filled with laughter, and our tongues with singing. Then they said among the nations, The Lord has done great things for them. The Lord has done great things for us! We are glad!" (Psalm 126:1-3 AMP). Ecclesiastes 3:4 says there is a time to laugh.

8. *Speaking about Him and His works* - **"I will extol thee, my God, O king; and I will bless thy name for ever and ever. Every day will I bless thee; and I will praise thy name for ever and ever. Great is the Lord, and greatly to be praised; and his greatness is unsearchable. One generation shall praise thy works to another, and shall declare thy mighty acts. I will speak of the glorious honour of thy majesty, and of thy wondrous works"** (Psalm 145:1-5).

9. *A joyful noise* - **"Make a joyful noise unto the Lord, all ye lands"** (Psalm 100:1). ("Making a joyful noise" is also mentioned in Psalm 66:1; 81:1; 95:1,2; 98:4,6.)

Psalm 16:11 says, **"...in thy presence is fulness of joy..."** Learn how to live in His presence. Become conscious of His presence within you. Also learn how to enter into the fellowship of His presence with thanksgiving and praise. Psalm 100:2,4 says, **"Serve the Lord with gladness: come before his presence with singing ... Enter into his gates with thanksgiving, and into his courts with praise: be thankful unto him, and bless his name."** Be a thankful person. (Note: Others will appreciate this also.)

If you've never known fullness of joy, then you don't know when you miss it. You can have fullness of joy from your right standing relationship with Jesus. It isn't just an experience in a church service. It is an established peace and freedom within. It is not having anything clogging up your "spiritual pipeline." It is where love prevails. It is where, with your faith, you are free from all guilt and condemnation of your past. It is where you have received freedom from inferiority and comparison with others. You have accepted your life in Christ and are thankful for Who He is inside of you. Oh, what a joy it is to be free in Jesus Christ!

Joy in Doing God's Will

There is joy in doing the will of God (Psalm 40:8). If you've lost your joy and peace, check to see where you possibly have stepped out from obeying the voice of God. God speaks to us in His written will, the Word of God, and gives us commands to walk in. He also speaks to us in our hearts by the "still small voice." He may direct you to do something that you may not want to do. He allows a person to choose whatever he or she wants to do. However, when a person goes his or her own way and refuses His direction, there is a sense of misery until he or she surrenders to His will. Once you are in His will, it is such a joy because of the peace it brings, even if it is in uncomfortable surroundings.

Sometimes in doing God's will, it is difficult at the moment, but there is a knowing in your spirit and an assurance of joy that will be ahead because of your obedience. For example, Hebrews 12:2 says, **"...for the joy that was set before him** [Jesus] **endured the cross, despising the same, and is set down at the right hand of the throne of God** [the highest position held]**."** He knew the joy of the harvest of lives that would be saved because of His obedience.

Verse 3 says to us as believers, to **"consider** [or think about, observe and take heed to] **him** [Jesus] **that endured such contradiction of sinners against himself, lest ye be wearied and faint in your minds** [become weak or shirk responsibility or lose consciousness in our own minds]**."** Being in God's will is one of the greatest joys you will ever experience.

Delighting in the Lord

Psalm 37:4 says, *"Delight thyself also in the Lord*; **and he shall give thee the desires of thine heart."** Learn how to delight in your relationship and fellowship with the Lord so that it isn't just a form of religion but a living relationship. Learn to enjoy the revelation of God's Word as you read it. Jeremiah 15:16 says, **"Thy words were found, and I did eat them; and thy word was unto me the joy and rejoicing of mine heart..."** Enjoy the Word so that you're not just in a habit of reading, but so you really get something out of it as you read it.

When we delight and joy in the Lord and in His Word, He will begin to bless us and give us the desires of our heart, because our desires start lining up with His desires. God is such a loving Father, He wants to bless us as His children. It is such a joy to Him when we love Him and enjoy Him. Any good earthly father would want to bless and do things for a child who sincerely loves him and enjoys being with him. It is even more so with our heavenly Father.

The Oil of Gladness

But unto the Son he saith, Thy throne, O God, is for ever and ever: a sceptre of righteousness is the sceptre of thy kingdom.

Thou hast loved righteousness, and hated iniquity; therefore God, even thy God, hath anointed thee with the oil of gladness above thy fellows.

And, Thou, Lord, in the beginning hast laid the foundation of the earth; and the heavens are the works of thine hands:

They shall perish; but thou remainest; and they all shall wax old as doth a garment;

And as a vesture shalt thou fold them up, and they shall be changed: but thou art the same, and thy years shall not fail.

Hebrews 1:8-12

Thy throne, O God, is for ever and ever: the scepter of thy kingdom is a right sceptre.

Thou lovest righteousness, and hatest wickedness: therefore God, thy God, hath anointed thee with the oil of gladness above thy fellows.

Psalm 45:6,7

Notice in Hebrews, chapter 1, verse 9, how God anointed His

Son Jesus with the oil of gladness. If Jesus has joy, then we have His joy within our hearts to draw upon. When Jesus opened the Scriptures to read in the temple (Luke 4:18), He read from Isaiah 61:1,2, which says:

> **The Spirit of the Lord God is upon me; because the Lord hath anointed me to preach good tidings unto the meek; he hath sent me to bind up the brokenhearted, to proclaim liberty to the captives, and the opening of the prison to them that are bound;**
>
> **To proclaim the acceptable year of the Lord, and the day of vengeance of our God; to comfort all that mourn.**

Jesus proclaimed that He was the Messiah and He had come to do all of these things He just read. Verse 3 goes on to say, **"To appoint** [place upon those who believe in Him as a permanent thing] **unto them that mourn in Zion, to give unto them beauty for ashes** [give them value], **the *oil of joy* for mourning** [joy to replace grief or shame]; ***the garment of praise* for the spirit of heaviness** [an attitude of praise and gratitude to replace being burdened, weak, faint, or depressed]; **that they might be called trees of righteousness** [in other words, be like strong oak trees], **the planting** [or establishing] **of the Lord, *that he might be glorified.*"**

Many times we've sung songs, such as "Lord, Be Glorified in My Life." He is glorified through our attitude of praise and gratefulness and our rejoicing in Him. If you need to shake off the oppression of the enemy (the devil), release anything that could be hindering you and begin to thank God that He is with you and He is mighty in your midst to save, deliver and rejoice over you with joy.

Zephaniah 3:17 says:

> **The Lord thy God in the midst of thee is mighty; he will save, he will rejoice over thee with joy; he will rest in his love, he will joy over thee with singing.**

Let the oil of the Holy Spirit be poured into and over your life.

He is your victory to overcome whatever you face. His joy is your strength, renewal and refreshing.

Endotes

[47] Dake, p. 207.
[48] Vine, p. 116.
[49] Webster, p. 1464.
[50] Vine, p. 836
[51] Ibid., p. 404.
[52] Ibid., p. 1167.
[53] Ibid., p. 608.
[54] Webster, p. 480.
[55] Charles Trombley, *Praise: Faith in Action,* Indianola, IA: Fountain Press, Inc., 1978, p. 25.

CHAPTER 7
PEACE

But the fruit of the Spirit is . . . peace

Galatians 5:22

I was driving down the street one day and saw a sign in front of a church that caught my attention. It read:

Know God – Know Peace;

No God – No Peace.

Isaiah 48:22 says, **"There is no peace, saith the Lord, unto the wicked."** People who live in sin do not have peace. For some, the reason is that they have an awareness that what they are doing is wrong. Some fear their sin could be found out and could damage their success or other relationships. Some live in fear that one day someone is going to "do them in" so they have to constantly think of keeping themselves in safe places. Others live in guilt or torment because of sin. Then some simply grow bitter over the years and try to drown their bitterness in one way or another.

Peace Comes By Being Right with God

Isaiah 32:17 says, **"...the effect of righteousness** [receiving God's gift of righteousness by faith and being right with God through faith in the cleansing blood of Jesus] **quietness and assurance for ever."** When a person realizes they can be right with God by *believing* in Jesus' blood to cleanse their sin, and by *confessing* that Jesus was raised from the dead and is their Lord and Savior, they can have *peace* within (Romans 8:9,10).

Romans 5:1 AMP says:

Therefore, since we are justified (acquitted, declared righteous, and given a right standing with God) through faith, let us [grasp the fact that we] have [the peace of reconciliation to hold and to enjoy] peace with God through our Lord Jesus Christ (the Messiah, the Anointed One).

No matter what sins are in your past or present, if you repent, turn from the sin and believe in Jesus' blood to cleanse you and walk in another direction, you are forgiven and cleansed as if you had never sinned (Isaiah 1:18; 1 John 1:9; Psalm 103:11,12).

Once you are free from the burden and guilt of sin, you are able to rise to the potential and the purpose God has for your life here on earth. Along with this comes the peace within that one day when you die physically, you'll continue to live spiritually and you'll simply change locations from earth to heaven. Some people live in fear of death because they don't know what is coming after they die.

There is good reason for their fear because those who don't receive Jesus and His cleansing blood here on earth will not go to heaven but to hell—torment forever. This is why it's so important to settle the questioning while there's time here on earth. Being totally surrendered to Jesus, believing and confessing Him as Lord and Savior, is your answer to receiving peace with God and knowing your eternal destination.

Peace with God Affects Peace with Your Surroundings

When you receive peace with God, it affects the way you relate to others. The opposite of peace is conflict, strife, violence, anger, confusion or disorder and fear. The peace of God brings freedom from these. Even though you may be around others who are in conflict or strife, confusion, fear, or anger, you can remain peaceful because the Prince of Peace (Jesus Christ) is living inside of you. All you have to do is draw on His presence through praying or worshipping God. You can even pray in your thoughts when you are surrounded by people who may be upset. God not only hears spoken prayers, but He also hears our thoughts.

Jesus - The Greatest Example of Peace

Jesus is your greatest example of total peace. In the account of Mark 4, Jesus was asleep in the boat with His disciples when the winds and waves began to swell to hurricane proportions. The disciples became fearful. They forgot that the Creator of the universe, the Son of Almighty God, the "all-sufficient One," was in the boat with them!

The disciples awoke Jesus and said to Him, **"...Master, do You not care that we are perishing?"** (Mark 4:38 AMP). In other words, "You should be worrying with us and at least lending a hand to bail the water out." They were not thinking that He could stop the storm.

Christians often react in the same way. We sometimes lose sight of the fact that the Son of God, the Son of the Highest, resides within us through the Holy Spirit. Many times we have prayed without really releasing any faith in God that He could change things—we have just prayed as a religious habit, still worrying after we prayed.

Jesus arose and rebuked the wind, saying, "Peace, be still." He then turned to the disciples and asked, "Why are you so fearful? How is it that you have no faith?" In the stormy situations of your life, turn your thoughts and prayers to Jesus, for He will *never* leave you nor forsake you! He is always present with you. Through Him you can use the authority He has invested in you and speak to the situations you face, saying, "peace, be still." Then cast the care on Him, and let Him carry it while you rest in His peace!

Heart Peace and Fear Don't Mix

Some people begin to dwell on all the negative things happening in the world around them and become fearful that something tragic will happen to them, such as disease, accidents, murder, etc. The person who does not have a right relationship and fellowship with the Lord doesn't have a peace within that God is with them and that He will keep those who put their faith in His Word (Psalm 91). Faith comes within our hearts as we hear and meditate God's Word (Romans 10:17). We have to guard our faith by guarding what we hear and meditate upon.

Isaiah 26:3 AMP says:

You will guard him and keep him in perfect and constant peace whose mind [both its inclination and its character] is stayed on You, because he commits himself to You, leans on You, and hopes confidently in You.

It's hard to trust and commit things to God and have peace unless you keep your mind from listening to thoughts of fear and worry.

I am frequently reminded of the memorable quote, "Fear knocked at the door. Faith answered, but no one was there!" Faith cannot operate when fear is present. Peace cannot be in control when fear is present either.

Where there is faith, there will be peace, even in the midst of the storms of life. Peace will prevail when you keep your mind upon the Word of God. Peace will prevail when you speak the Word of God over situations that exist in your life—and watch the situations move while you remain stable (standing still)! Find the promises in the Bible on *peace*. Write them out, then pray them over your life and your situations.

Philippians 4:6,7 AMP says:

Do not fret or have any anxiety about anything, but in every circumstance and in everything, by prayer and petition (definite requests), with thanksgiving, continue to make your wants known to God.

And God's peace [shall be yours, that tranquil state of a soul assured of its salvation through Christ, and so fearing nothing from God and being content with its earthly lot of whatever sort that is, that peace] which

transcends all understanding shall garrison and mount guard over your hearts and minds in Christ Jesus.

When God's peace mounts guard over your heart and mind, none of the fiery darts of the enemy will be able to hurt you. They may still come, but the peace of God within you will repel them!

Jesus is speaking to you and me in John 14:27 AMP when He says:

Peace I leave with you; My [own] peace I now give and bequeath to you. Not as the world gives do I give to you. Do not let your hearts be troubled, neither let them be afraid. [Stop allowing yourselves to be agitated and disturbed; and do not permit yourselves to be fearful and intimidated and cowardly and unsettled.]

Jesus is saying, "DON'T *ALLOW* THE HEART PEACE WHICH I HAVE FREELY GIVEN YOU AS MY CHILD BE UPSET, DISTURBED, CONFUSED, INTIMIDATED, OR FEARFUL IN ANY WAY. BUT *LET* THE HEART PEACE WHICH I HAVE PLACED WITHIN YOU AND ABOUT YOU DOMINATE YOU IN ALL SITUATIONS!" The responsibility for staying in peace, for letting peace dominate, and for letting God's peace continue to grow, falls upon you and me! We will either allow fear, worry, confusion, or strife to control us, or we will choose to focus our thoughts on His Word which produces peace.

In Philippians 4:6 AMP we read, **"Do not fret or have any anxiety about anything. . . ."** The understood subject is *you*. You are not to worry about anything. *Anything* means anything! **"...but *in* every circumstance and *in* everything, by prayer and petition (definite requests), with thanksgiving, continue to make your wants known to God."** Pray God's Word over the matter because He answers His own Word (1 John 5:14,15). *Petition* means to ask God for the need you are facing. Then, thank Him after you've asked in faith and prayed Scripture relating to it, even before you see any answer.

Many people ask God for things, but they don't ask Him with the Scripture and do not release their faith that He heard their prayer. Furthermore, they don't thank God immediately after they've prayed. They think they are to wait until they see something before they thank Him. Faith believes before it sees anything (Mark 11:24). After praying with thanksgiving, there is a peace that God is taking care of it all. That peace is what Philippians 4:7 describes as a wall around our thoughts. It is a quiet assurance that God is faithful to keep His promises (Hebrews 10:23).

I remember when our second daughter was a baby and we had been given some negative reports regarding her health. My husband and I took the Scripture and immediately began speaking it over her life. We had to place her in the hospital at the same time we had been told the possible diagnosis. We were grateful to all the medical people who worked with her, but we kept our faith on the confession of God's Word instead of on the possible diagnosis.

Within twenty-four hours, they ruled out two dangerous diagnoses and then we stood on the Word of God for ten months until the other diagnosis was proven wrong. Thank God. In the midst of it all, we felt that the Word kept us in a cocoon of peace and grace.

God's Peace and the World's Peace Differ

God's peace is eternal, while the world's peace is only momentary. People who are not saved seek peace by going on vacations or going to peaceful places. Vacations and times of getting away are good, but it's not always possible. Sometimes people get momentary peace through drugs, etc., but drugs only enslave a person. If we are anchored into Christ Jesus and the Word of God, we can learn to draw on the presence of God and His peace in the midst of any situation. We choose not to become troubled or afraid when trouble comes. It doesn't mean that trouble will not come around, but if it comes, you can choose to respond with faith in God's Word. You don't have to accept something negative and become overwhelmed by it.

The world is filled with instability and troubles in the form of wars, unemployment, crimes, famines, bizarre weather conditions, and turmoil, but Jesus is saying to you and me today, **"I have told you these things, so that in Me you may have [perfect] peace and confidence. In the world you have tribulation and trials and distress and frustration; but be of good cheer [take courage; be confident, certain, undaunted]! For *I have overcome the world. [I have deprived it of power to harm you and have conquered it for you]*"** (John 16:33 AMP).

When we look at the life of Daniel, the world about him was everything but peaceful. Daniel and the other young Hebrew men were taken as slaves to Babylon after Jerusalem was destroyed. Because these men sought God, He favored them. Daniel was anointed with wisdom, and he had an excellent spirit (Daniel 1:20; 6:3).

In Daniel 6, we read that there were those who were jealous of Daniel and conspired against him. Because they could not find fault with Daniel, they devised a scheme to get the king to make a decree that any person who petitioned any god or man other than the king would be thrown to the lions. They knew Daniel prayed three times a day in petition to God and knew that they could catch him.

Daniel, however, continued to pray and seek his God openly. He was then brought before the king to be charged for not obeying this decree. The king liked Daniel above the others, but because his signet was on the decree, he had no choice but to honor the decree and throw Daniel into the lions' den.

The king spent a sleepless night, with no peace, being in great fear for Daniel. However, Daniel was fully confident in God's hand of deliverance.

Notice, in this situation Daniel's peace was not because of comfortable surroundings. Quite the contrary! He was in an impossible situation from the natural point of view!

However, the king was the one who could not sleep for fear, even though he was in the most comfortable surroundings in the entire kingdom—the palace—with the best bed in the kingdom. Here we see that peace is not a *place*, but a state of being. You can be on the most beautiful beach away from people and noise, but if you are in fear or you have strife over some situation, you will not have peace. Also, notice that Daniel kept his peace toward those trying to hurt him. He let God handle the whole situation. Don't let fear and anger rob your peace.

Even in the midst of great responsibility or demands upon your life, if you take time with God daily, He will enable you to walk in peace and give you wisdom for handling everything. He can help you balance your responsibilities or delegate things that are not necessary for you to do. He can help you prioritize your life and show you how to do what you can do, then leave the results in His hands. In other words, He can show you how to walk in His peace and rest, free of worry, in the midst of a lot of things going on (1 Peter 5:7; Hebrews 4:3).

Jesus walked in peace in spite of the great demands placed upon Him. The masses surrounded Him constantly. There were times, however, when Jesus stepped aside from the masses of people into a solitary place to spend time in prayer, *maintaining His intimate relationship* with the Father.

Years ago while I was in prayer, the Spirit of God spoke to my heart and said, "Come apart, Sharon, before you come apart." So I know there are times when you must step aside from the busy daily routines and go to a place of solitude to receive from the Lord. This time is never wasted time! Instead, through time with Him, God will set your pace for the day and restore your soul with peace.

Psalm 23:2,3 says, **"...he leadeth me beside the still waters. He restoreth my soul."** We all need our souls restored daily. If we don't take time with Him alone daily, it will begin to show by our attitude becoming "edgy" with the people around us. We won't be as sensitive to the fact that we spoke too quickly or too sharply with someone. We will be more prone to worry or be fretful. Time with the Lord helps us be more watchful in our attitudes, words and actions. Peace becomes more important to us than holding offenses or worrying.

Be a Peacemaker

Blessed are the peacemakers: for they shall be called the children of God.

Matthew 5:9

In a world of strife and violence, God's Word says that we are to be peacemakers. Romans 12:18 says, **"...as much as lieth in you, live peaceably with all men."** Obviously, not all people will live at peace toward you, but you are to live at peace with and toward them. You choose not to enter into strife and arguments.

Sometimes you can walk out of a strife-filled room. At other times you may have to stand in the midst of it, but hold your peace. Arguments require more than one person speaking. You can choose not to speak. It doesn't mean that the other person wins. In fact, it proves who is stronger in character and in leadership. You'll find most people will follow a peaceful person rather than a strife-filled person, because they trust their stability. An angry and easily agitated person is unstable and cannot be trusted in what they might do out of an emotional whim. They only have followers because of fear and intimidation. Someone who does not take control over their emotions is not walking in fellowship with Jesus. Even though they may say that they are a Christian, their behavior says something else. Our attitudes and actions speak as loud as our words.

Sometimes to avoid strife, a person must choose to let someone else have their choice in a matter. This does not mean that the person who gives up their desire will be at a loss. God always rewards peacemakers who walk in faith.

In Genesis 13 when Abraham had left his father and the land of Ur of the Chaldees, Lot his nephew wanted to go with him. Abraham allowed him to follow. Both men had many servants and livestock. As they journeyed, Lot's servants got into strife with Abraham's servants. Abraham went to Lot and said, "To have no strife between us, you decide which direction you want to go and the land where you want to settle." Abraham agreed to go the opposite direction to another place.

Lot chose the most fertile land in which to settle, Sodom and Gomorrah. After he made his choice, God told Abraham to look to the east, the west, the north and the south, and said, "I'm going to give it all to you."

Lot found that Sodom and Gomorrah were full of wickedness. He stayed there until right before they were destroyed. He escaped with his wife and daughters because of Abraham's prayer for him. However, his wife was so attached to the place that she looked back with longing and turned into a pillar of salt. The attitude of Sodom and Gomorrah had gotten into Lot's whole family.

The day came when Abraham and his seed inherited all of the promised land (Israel). When we have a peacemaker attitude in resolving conflict, ultimately we will win.

Hebrews 12:14 says, **"Follow peace with all men, and holiness, without which no man shall see the Lord."** The Greek word for *follow after* is *dioko*, meaning to pursue; chase after; seek after; follow closely.[56] Peace does not just happen. You must continually pursue it.

In order to pursue peace, you have to choose not to hold offense. Jesus said offenses are going to come our way (Luke 17:1). By a choice we can release them and let them go. Our own forgiveness from God depends on our forgiving other people (Mark 11:25). If we choose ahead of time to be a forgiving person, when the opportunity comes to be hurt and offended, we will be able to let it go more easily.

When I found the scripture in Psalm 119:165 – **"Great peace have they which love thy law: and nothing shall offend them"** – I realized I had to put the Word of God in me *daily* to keep myself from holding offenses. I found that when offenses came, the Word of God and the Holy Spirit would convict me to release them and let God have them. Ultimately, things would turn for my good, and most of all, I remained free and peaceful.

The Scripture does tell us how to handle an offense if it is necessary to confront another person to resolve a matter:

Moreover if thy brother shall trespass against thee, go and tell him his fault between thee and him alone: if he shall hear thee, thou hast gained thy brother.

But if he will not hear thee, then take with thee one or two more, that in the mouth of two or three witnesses every word may be established.

And if he shall neglect to hear them, tell it unto the church: but if he neglect to hear the church, let him be unto thee as an heathen man and a publican.

Verily I say unto you, Whatsoever ye shall bind on earth shall be bound in heaven: and whatsoever ye shall loose on earth shall be loosed in heaven.

Matthew 18:15-18

First, we are to go privately to the individual. If he or she listens and wants to explain and resolve it, then you are released to go on and not hold a grudge.

If they do not want to resolve it, then take another person with you to speak to them. If they still want to hold on to their offense and not resolve it, then go to the leadership of the church. Then the leadership can speak with them in order to resolve it. If they will not listen to the church leadership, then you are to treat them as you would treat an unbeliever. This means, love them from a distance and pray for them to change, but you are no longer responsible to have close fellowship with them.

Most Christians, when offended, want to go to a friend first and talk about the person who offended them. Then some Christians want to go to church leadership first and make them resolve it. There is an order that Jesus gave for us to handle offenses properly. Sometimes Christians who are fearful have difficulty going to others. The Holy Spirit wants us to lovingly confront when we need to. Before going to someone else, it is important that we examine our own lives so we go in the right spirit or attitude.

Matthew 7:3-5 says:

And why beholdest thou the mote that is in thy brother's eye, but considerest not the beam that is in

thine own eye?

Or how wilt thou say to thy brother, Let me pull out the mote out of thine eye; and, behold, a beam is in thine own eye?

Thou hypocrite, first cast out the beam out of thine own eye; and then shalt thou see clearly to cast out the mote out of thy brother's eye.

Once you've asked God to forgive you of wrong attitudes or actions, then go to the person in a spirit of humility and talk to him or her about the offense that happened.

Let Peace Direct Your Life

"**And let the peace of Christ act as umpire** [in your life]" (*Rotherham's Translation* of Colossians 3:15). *The Amplified Bible* says it this way:

And let the peace (soul harmony which comes) from Christ rule (act as umpire continually) in your hearts [deciding and settling with finality all questions that arise in your minds, in that peaceful state] to which as [members of Christ's] one body you were also called [to live]. And be thankful (appreciative), [giving praise to God always].

An umpire in a softball game makes all of the final decisions on the plays. In seeking direction from God, the peace of God will reign when you are on the right path. His peace will guide you in making final decisions and handling situations you are not sure about.

There are times when you will "know that you know that you know" the direction you are to take. At other times, you will have that inside witness of stopping your plan of action. Then there are times you will not have a direction. His peace will guide you to cautiously proceed, ready to stop if necessary, examining yourself and the situation. This is how you are directed by the inner peace.

Sometimes time is needed to settle your heart with His peace.

Most of us want big signs to tell us to stop or go. In 1 Kings 19, Elijah went to be alone, hoping to hear from God. God told him to stand on the mountain. As Elijah stood, the Lord caused a great, strong wind to blow and break pieces of rock. Then an earthquake came. Next, there was a fire, but the Lord wasn't in any of these three notable signs. Instead, He spoke in a still, small voice to Elijah.

God wants us to learn to listen to and trust the still, small voice within our hearts. We can judge our thoughts and directives by God's Word. God's leading of peace will remain, even as time passes. Putting God's Word in us is like constantly improving our "gauge" or "measuring stick." As time passes, we will grow in our ability to hear and discern His voice in our hearts by the measuring rod of His *peace*.

Endotes

[56] Vine, p. 442.

CHAPTER 8
LONGSUFFERING

But the fruit of the Spirit is . . . longsuffering [patience]
Galatians 5:22

Webster defines longsuffering as "long and patient endurance of injuries, insults and trouble; patiently bearing difficulties or wrongs."[57] *Moffatt's Translation* says longsuffering is "being good tempered." *Phillips' Translation* calls it "patience."

In a society that is dominated more and more by "instant" products, we have to consciously make an effort to develop longsuffering or patience. For example, we are so accustomed to instant coffee, instant pudding, instant potatoes, instant meals in a microwave oven, instant success, instant money. However, life doesn't always hand us instant answers. This is why patience is so vital to receive the promises of God. Patience [longsuffering] is the fruit that enables us to wait and not demand our own way. When we have a demanding attitude, we are prone to give up quickly and blame God.

One of God's characteristics or attributes is that He is longsuffering. Exodus 34:6 says, **"...The Lord God, merciful and gracious, *longsuffering*, and abundant in goodness and truth."** First Peter 3:20 tells us that though the world was full of wickedness in the days of Noah, God in His longsuffering waited for years as Noah preached to the people while he prepared an ark of safety for himself and his family, hoping the people would turn to God. The children of Israel are another example of God's longsuffering toward mankind. Through the years, the Old Testament reveals how they failed over and over again to keep the laws of God. Yet each time they cried out to God and repented of their sin, God in His infinite love, mercy and longsuffering delivered them.

Every Christian has failed God in some way at some time in his life. Yet God always extends His loving forgiveness and forbearance to you when you repent and turn again to Him. The reason is that He loves mankind so much and wants a relationship with man, but He will not force anyone to love and obey Him. Our love and obedience must be voluntary. God wants us to love Him by our choice. He has given people time, warning and mercy over and over again. However, sometimes the devil cuts lives short so they never receive Jesus and they go into eternity damned. This is not God's plan for man. However, He gives us freedom of choice.

In the book of Jonah, God chose to extend His mercy and longsuffering to Nineveh. That's why He sent Jonah to warn of coming judgment if they didn't repent. Jonah despised the Lord's longsuffering and goodness to the people of Nineveh. He wanted them to be punished for their sins. After going through the fish experience, he was ready to warn them. Once he had warned them, he went to sit and watch what would happen. God caused a plant to grow up to shade him, then allowed it to die. Jonah became upset because the plant died. God then asked him, "Do you have more mercy for a plant than for human beings?" Because they had responded to His warning and repented, shouldn't He have mercy on them? He was trying to help Jonah to see that He had mercy on him as well as on Nineveh.

Romans 2:4 says that we are not to despise the goodness, forbearance, and longsuffering of God, knowing that the goodness of God leads men to repentance.

The Lord is not slack concerning his promise, as some men count slackness; but is longsuffering to usward, not willing that any should perish, but that all should come to repentance.

2 Peter 3:9

God's will for mankind is to save them even though not everyone will receive Jesus and let Him in their hearts so that they can be saved. This is why He has waited to return to earth, because He desires to see a great harvest of souls saved before that appointed time.

Second Peter 3:15 says, **"...the longsuffering of our Lord is salvation."** Thank God for His patience toward us and toward the world today.

James 5:7,8 says:

Be patient therefore, brethren, unto the coming of the Lord. Behold, the husbandman waiteth for the precious fruit of the earth, and hath long patience for it, until he receive the early and latter rain.

Be ye also patient; stablish your hearts: for the coming of the Lord draweth nigh.

Be Patient Toward All Men

First Thessalonians 5:14 says, **"...be patient toward all men."** Just as God is patient, we as His children are called to be patient toward others. When the Scripture says "be patient toward *all* men," that includes the saved and the unsaved. *All* is all. It means all mankind. We're commanded to be patient with everyone.

Believe me, I've been around people at times who seem to thrive on pushing others to react negatively. It takes a deliberate decision to respond in peace toward them.

And the servant of the Lord must not strive; but be gentle unto all men, apt to teach, patient,

In meekness instructing those who oppose themselves; if God peradventure will give them repentance to the acknowledging of the truth;

And that they may recover themselves out of the snare of the devil, who are taken captive by him at his will.

2 Timothy 2:24-26

Patience will keep you from striving with others. Frustration, strife and anger will not change another person, but patience will create an atmosphere for them to feel convicted to change. First Corinthians 13:4 says that love suffers long. If we walk in the agape, unconditional love (the love that is in spite of), patience (longsuffering) will be a natural by-product.

Being patient will require your feelings to suffer at times. First Peter 2:20 says:

For what glory is it, if, when ye be buffeted for your faults, ye shall take it patiently? but if, when ye do well, and suffer for it, ye take it patiently, this is acceptable with God.

Your feelings will want to strike back when someone speaks or acts wrongly or falsely accuses you or persecutes you. Your feelings will want to simply give up and walk away from those who are not doing as they should.

When my husband and I were in college years ago, there was a particular guy who appeared to dislike my husband. Since they were in a lot of activities and classes together and in the same dorm, they saw each other often. My husband prayed for him. We ended up changing colleges and never saw him again. Years later while holding a series of evangelistic meetings in a town, we received a phone call from this same man who was a head coach at the public school there. He invited my husband to come and share his testimony with the athletes.

When he introduced my husband, he shared how he had observed Billy Joe at college and watched his witness of Jesus Christ. He shared how it had impacted his life to receive Jesus as his own Lord and Savior, which he did after we had transferred to the other college.

Sometimes we're called to live our witness with patience with others who may appear to be resistant at the moment, but later surrender to the love of God.

A lady in our church shared in a testimony how that for twenty years in her marriage relationship she had prayed for her husband to be saved. She went to church through those years when he would not go. One day she heard how to pray scriptures about what she desired to see in her husband. She prayed 1 Timothy 2:24 that he would be saved and come to a knowledge of the truth. She bound the god of this world from blinding his eyes (Matthew 18:18; 2 Corinthians 4:4). She prayed that the eyes of his understanding would be enlightened (Ephesians 1:17-19). She prayed he would become the spiritual head of their household according to Ephesians 5:23-33 and that he would love her and the family like Christ loves the Church.

It was not long after praying the Scriptures that he came to church with her and walked forward at the invitation, giving his life to Jesus Christ. Her patience and standing on God's Word paid off. God's love within a person doesn't give up but believes His Word is working in the lives of those for whom they are praying.

Paul tells us in Colossians 3:14 that love is the bond of perfectness which binds people together. Longsuffering is like a tough fiber which keeps this love bond from breaking under stress and strain. All relationships will at times experience stress and strain, but the fruit of longsuffering will keep the bond intact.

Longsuffering is essential to a healthy marriage relationship or to any relationship. I've heard of many marriages being dissolved on the grounds of what is called "incompatibility." *Incompatibility* is simply when two people demand their own way. It is when two people will not adjust to one another and make an effort to resolve differences. They choose not to love one another in spite of. We've all been incompatible at times, but if we will let the Spirit of Jesus take control, we can learn to be compatible, to adjust and to meet each other's needs.

I have a very compatible relationship with my husband, but we've had to work at it. There have been times when selfishness, differences of opinion, stress and strain have come against us, but we have chosen not to let these dictate our emotions and destroy us. Instead, we made a decision years ago to love each other in spite of our differences, to adjust and to love by faith at times when our feelings were not happy about everything. Determination coupled with God's grace and strength can do a lot for a marriage.

Communication is a key to growth in a loving relationship. A friend of ours once said, "Frustration ends where communication begins." Any strong marriage is a marriage where two people have learned to talk and share openly with one another without becoming hostile. It is having self-control and the desire to listen to and understand each other.

Those who are good leaders are people who have sought to understand others and be patient when others don't always meet their expectations. Remember, what you sow you will reap. If you want others to be understanding and patient with you, then you must be understanding and patient toward them.

Patience requires us to "go the extra mile" with people at times (Matthew 5:41).

Acts 15:35-41 tells us how Paul and Barnabas traveled together in ministry and brought along a young man named Mark to mentor. Mark, being young and immature, frustrated Paul. Paul decided he did not want Mark traveling with them. Barnabas, who had reached out to Paul when others were cautious toward him, decided that he would take Mark and travel another direction to spread the Gospel. Paul took Silas, and he and Barnabas parted ways.

Barnabas, at this time, had more longsuffering than Paul with younger ministers. Later in Scripture, Paul realized how Mark had grown spiritually because of Barnabas not giving up on him. Paul then sent for Mark to come and help him. Paul grew in patience as he continued to minister to people.

In 2 Corinthians 6:4 Paul says that we approve ourselves as ministers of the Lord in having much patience. (See also 1 Timothy 3:3; Titus 2:2.)

Sometimes patience requires us to love or do good to people

who may not like us. Matthew 5:43-48 says:

Ye have heard that it hath been said, Thou shalt love thy neighbour, and hate thine enemy.

But I say unto you, Love your enemies, bless them that curse you, do good to them that hate you, and pray for them which despitefully use you, and persecute you;

That ye may be the children of your Father which is in heaven: for he maketh his sun to rise on the evil and on the good, and sendeth rain on the just and on the unjust.

For if ye love them which love you, what reward have ye? do not even the publicans the same?

And if ye salute your brethren only, what do ye more than others? do not even the publicans so?

Be ye therefore perfect, even as your Father which is in heaven is perfect.

Remember, nothing can stop the love of God. Ultimately, it will win and you will be like your Father God.

Patience in Trials and Tests of Faith

The fruit of patience (longsuffering) is needed when you are going through a trial or test of your faith. Patience is not developed by the trial itself, but when you allow the Word of God to be your focus during this time, patience will grow and mature in your life. Some have said that trials and tribulations develop patience and make us strong Christians. The problem with that thought is that some people who have gone through trials have turned away from God instead of to God. *Trials and tribulations do not necessarily develop patience! However, if a person focuses their attention on God's Word and keeps himself or herself standing in prayer, they will develop patience.* It basically comes down to our attitude to stand firm and believe God's Word during the test.

James 1:4 says when we learn to rejoice in the midst of a trial or test, the trying of our faith will work patience. If we let patience have her perfect work, we will be perfect and entire, wanting nothing. James is not saying to be joyful *because* we are tempted, tested, or tried. He is saying, however, that *in the midst of* temptations, tests, and trials, we should rejoice in the Lord.

Godly longsuffering does not mean that you simply resign yourself to a position or an attitude of "I must just endure." The God-kind of longsuffering is not merely an endurance; rather, it is standing and maintaining an attitude of joy and a vision of God's Word perfecting everything that concerns you. You see it as another opportunity for the Word of God to prevail in your life.

The difference between endurance and godly longsuffering is the fruit of joy. In Colossians 1:11, Paul prayed that we would be **strengthened with all might, according to his glorious power, unto all patience and longsuffering with *joyfulness*.** The joy of the Lord will be your strength to stand with patience in the trial.

Some people go through trials with a "poor little 'ol me" attitude. This attitude doesn't glorify God. Godly longsuffering will not bring attention to self but will glorify God and point others to His grace and power.

James says if we let patience have her complete work, not giving up too soon, we will be fully developed in that test, passing it and lacking in nothing by the end of the trial.

Romans 5:3-5 says that we glory in tribulation (we rejoice in the midst of testing), knowing that the test works patience and patience works experience (victory and proof that God will perform His promises if we believe); and experience works hope (hope that if we ever face another test or trial in the future, God will work another victory again); and hope makes not ashamed (we will not be defeated or shamed but victorious), because the love of God is shed abroad in our hearts by the Holy Ghost which is given unto us. (We grow in greater understanding of the love of God in our lives because of the power of the Holy Spirit.)

Dake says, "We have grace to endure trials without sustaining loss or deterioration. We are like silver and gold when refined."[58] Instead of loss, we will shine brighter after the trial.

The Scripture says we've been surrounded by a great cloud of witnesses (those saints who have gone on before us), who have stood on God's Word (Hebrews 12:1). Hebrews 6:12 says, **"...be not slothful, but followers of them who through *faith* and *patience* inherit the promises."** Faith coupled with patience will bring the fulfillment of God's Word in your life. Faith believes in what cannot be seen with the natural eye. Faith takes God's Word as final authority and stands. The spirit of faith believes and speaks what God's Word says, instead of what circumstances seem to be saying.

> **Let us hold fast the profession of our faith without wavering; (for he is faithful that promised).**
>
> **Hebrews 10:23**

Obviously, God sees that we need patience. When life is easy, we do not have to grow in patience. However, when we have to stand on God's Word and act on it in faith, then we grow in patience so we are better equipped to accomplish whatever God tells us to do.

The prayer Paul prayed in Colossians 1:9-11 was that we would **"...be filled with the knowledge of his will in all wisdom and spiritual understanding; that ye might walk worthy of the Lord unto all pleasing, being fruitful in every good work, and increasing in the knowledge of God; strengthened with all might, according to his glorious power, *unto all patience and longsuffering with joyfulness.*"**

Patience [longsuffering] is part of walking worthy of the Lord, pleasing to Him and to others. It strengthens us and enables us to be fruitful in every good work and to increase in our knowledge of God.

Endotes

[57] Webster, p. 834.
[58] Dake, p. 164.

91

CHAPTER 9
GENTLENESS

But the fruit of the Spirit is . . . gentleness

Galatians 5:22

Webster defines *gentleness* as "being *kind*, serene, patient, *not harsh*, violent, or rough."[59] Note how all of these qualities describe God's character.

Psalm 117:1,2 says, **"O praise the Lord, all ye nations: praise him, all ye people. For his *merciful kindness* is great toward us. . . ."** Ephesians 2:7 says, **"That in the ages to come he might shew the exceeding riches of his grace in his *kindness* toward us *through Christ Jesus.*"**

Titus 3:3-5 says:

> **For we ourselves also were sometimes foolish, disobedient, deceived, serving divers lusts and pleasures, living in malice and envy, hateful, and hating one another.**
>
> **But after that the *kindness* and love of God our Saviour toward man appeared ... according to his mercy he saved us....**

Even though God has set principles that, if broken, have their own payment, He wants us to walk in His blessings (Deuteronomy 30:19,20). He will work with us in spite of our weaknesses as long as we see our need for His help and allow Him to work in our lives.

The psalmist David realized this. He admitted his failures and his need, and he sought after the Lord. Psalm 18:35 is a quote from

David: **"Thou hast also given me the shield of thy salvation: and thy right hand hath holden me up [sustained me], and thy *gentleness* hath made me great."** (See also 2 Samuel 22:36.) David knew his source of greatness was not in himself but in his relationship to his kind and merciful God. In spite of David's sin, God said he was a man after His own heart (1 Samuel 13:14; Acts 13:22).

I like Donald Gee's description of gentleness in his book, *Fruit of the Spirit*: strength or power under perfect control. Since Jesus said that if you've seen Him you've seen the Father, we can look at His life and understand what God is like. Jesus had great strength and power, but it was always under the control of the Holy Spirit. Jesus had the ability to call upon powerful angelic legions to annihilate enemies, but He didn't. He had supernatural power to destroy, but He didn't. Acts 10:38 says, **"[He] went about doing good, and healing all that were oppressed of the devil."** That is the character of God. He treated people with love. He loved sinners and those who felt unworthy and gave them value and worth.

Jesus' Example of Gentleness

Notice Jesus' gentleness toward the woman who was caught in adultery (John 8:1-11).

The Pharisees, attempting to catch Jesus in error of the law, asked Him whether this woman ought to be stoned. He ignored them for a time. Then He stood up, and with great composure said to them, **"He that is without sin among you, let him first cast a stone at her"** (John 8:7). They departed one by one. Only Jesus and the accused woman remained. Jesus asked her, **"Woman, where are those thine accusers? hath no man condemned thee?"** (v. 10). She answered, **"No man, Lord"** (v. 11). Although He had the right to condemn her, for He was without sin, Jesus responded in gentleness (with deep compassion from His heart), **"Neither do I condemn thee: go, and sin no more"** (v. 11). He was the first gentleman she had ever met. What an impact He had upon her life!

Jesus never condoned sin, but He always ministered His love toward the people held in its bondage. Jesus said that He came not to condemn the world, but to save it (John 3:17). He came to show us the effects of sin that destroy and the goodness of God's salvation that saves and heals.

Jesus admonished the woman tenderly to go and sin no more. People had always been harsh with her and had taken advantage of her, but that day she was touched by the kind mercy of God through Jesus Christ and her life was changed. Now there was motivation to live a new kind of life.

If the church condemns and has no compassion for sinners, they will not be drawn to Jesus. We are called to go after sinners like Jesus went after us. We are called to love and encourage when people fall. We are to pick them up and say, "Go on and leave the past behind; you can walk in a newness of life; don't stay down; get up again; God still loves you and He'll help you."

Gentleness Toward Others

Because of his great concern for their souls, Paul instructed people with the meekness and gentleness of Christ to hear the word of the Lord (2 Corinthians 10:1). If we are going to reconcile people, we must have true compassion and make every effort to help people see their need with the spirit of humility and gentleness. If we would pause and think, when we needed correction, we would want others to treat us in this way, and it would affect how we relate to others.

A good father will discipline his children, but he knows that harshness and anger can destroy a child emotionally and create anger within him or her that will destroy others when they grow older. He realizes he must help them see their error as he instructs them with gentleness. (Note: Discipline with the rod is acceptable according to Scripture, but anger with it is not acceptable. Discipline should build character, not destroy it.)

Proverbs 22:15 says, **"Foolishness is bound in the heart of a child; but the rod of correction shall drive it far from him."** However, the writer of Proverbs also said, **"He that is slow to anger is better than the mighty; and he that ruleth his spirit than he that taketh a city"** (Proverbs 16:32). Conquering your inner self and controlling your emotions make you stronger and greater, even than someone who has conquered a city in battle. I might add, while some focus much attention on becoming stronger in the muscles of their bodies, they could help those around them if they also became stronger in their ability to control themselves emotionally.

The servant of the Lord must know how to correct or instruct with the spirit of gentleness so as not to destroy but to build others' lives.

Gentleness and patience *always* change people, while striving with people never changes them. Harshness or anger drives a wedge or builds a wall between people so they cannot hear the truth that can set them free. We're to build bridges with others so they can walk across and find the way out of their sin, their bondage, or the pit of life that they are in.

And the servant of the Lord must not be quarrelsome (fighting and contending). Instead, he must be kindly to everyone and *mild-tempered* [preserving the bond of peace]; he must be a skilled and suitable teacher, patient and forbearing and willing to suffer wrong.

He must correct his opponents with courtesy and *gentleness*, in the hope that God may grant that they will repent and come to know the Truth [that they will perceive and recognize and become accurately acquainted with and acknowledge it],

And that they may come to their senses [and] escape out of the snare of the devil, having been held captive by him, [henceforth] to do His [God's] will.

2 Timothy 2:24-26 AMP

Notice, Paul says we must be mild-tempered with people.

Ecclesiastes 3:1 says, **"To every thing there is a season, and a time to every purpose under the heaven."** Matthew 11:12 says, **"...the violent take it** [the kingdom of heaven] **by force."** Jesus was speaking of being spiritually zealous for God and violent against the demonic powers. Through prayer, we can bind the demonic power and loose people to receive God's grace. Let your forcefulness and violence be used constructively in the Spirit to pray God's Word and enforce your authority over the devil. In this way, you will avoid hurting people.

Many times people have no idea that they are being manipulated by demonic powers. Through prayer we have authority over Satan and his demons to stop their work in people's lives. Then how we handle the people should be by the leading of the Holy Spirit and compassion.

We must have such a compassion for people that we are willing not only to impart the Gospel of Jesus Christ into their lives, but to pour our very lives into them. Compassion compels us to help them overcome weaknesses of the flesh and to renew their minds to think according to the Word of God, thus causing them to walk differently than they've walked before.

But we behaved *gently* when we were among you, like a devoted mother nursing and cherishing her own children.

So, being thus tenderly and affectionately desirous of you, we continued to share with you not only God's good news (the Gospel) but also our own lives as well, for you had become so very dear to us.

1 Thessalonians 2:7,8 AMP

Helping Others Walk

When a toddler is learning to walk, he will fall down many times. A good parent, however, doesn't scold him for falling. He or she will pick him up, set him on his feet and tell him to try again. The parent repeatedly encourages and reassures him until the toddler is able to walk without falling. Likewise, babes in Christ may take a few tumbles as they are learning to walk with God. The mature believers must be encouragers, lifting them with the Word and the love of God, telling them, "You can do it. Get up and walk again."

Behold, My Servant Whom I have chosen, My Beloved in and with Whom My soul is well pleased and has found its delight. I will put My Spirit upon Him, and He shall proclaim and show forth justice to the nations.

He will not strive or wrangle or cry out loudly; nor will anyone hear His voice in the streets;

A bruised reed He will not break, and a smoldering (dimly burning) wick He will not quench, till He brings justice and a just cause to victory.

Matthew 12:18-20 AMP

The bruised reed and the smoking flax represent weak, young Christians who are not yet established in their faith. They may still have some traits that present difficulties in walking the Christian life. Jesus will not discourage, reject, or cast them away, but He will lift people's eyes to see there is a better life than what they have lived. Jesus needs you and me to be His hands to lift them, His voice to instruct and encourage, His feet to go after them, His heart to understand and His arms to surround them with compassion.

Gentleness Does Not Eliminate Correction, Rebuke and Instruction

Being gentle does not mean we are not to be lovingly firm and straightforward at times when it is needed. Jesus addressed wrong attitudes and actions. Paul also addressed the churches of Rome, Corinth, Galatia, Ephesus, and others on wrong attitudes and actions. However, underlying their words of instruction, you sense that they really cared for the people they were addressing. Their words were a loving rebuke and instruction on what to do.

Paul even says in Ephesians 4:29, **"Let no corrupt communication proceed out of your mouth, but that which is good to the use of** *edifying*, **that it may minister grace unto the hearers."** To *edify* means "to build; establish; to instruct or improve morally and spiritually."[60]

Words and the attitude behind those words can either destroy or build. They can create love or hate, forgiveness and peace or anger and resentment. One reason we have violent criminals is because of the harsh words and actions shown to them as children. How powerful are words and attitudes? Powerful enough to start wars and destroy lives, but also powerful enough to create peacemakers, great leaders, godly husbands and godly wives.

If you've been in a habit of speaking negatively or destructively, you can change right now. Repent and ask God to cleanse you with the blood of Jesus. Now, ask Him to help you with your words and attitudes. Renew your mind by reading and praying scriptures over your life daily. Proverbs 23:7 says, **"For as he thinketh in his heart, so is he...."** You'll become what you meditate on. Matthew 12:34 says, **"...out of the abundance of the heart the mouth speaketh."** Whatever you are putting in your mind and heart will be what you speak to others.

Wise As Serpents, Gentle As Doves

Jesus said that His children should be as *wise* as serpents and as *harmless* (gentle, guileless, and innocent) as doves (Matthew 10:16). In one sense, we are to be wise like the serpent who does not expose himself to attack. The serpent is cautious, sharpsighted, discerning, and knowing. Jesus implied that His children are also to be cautious, sharpsighted, discerning, and knowing.

James 3:17,18 says:

But the wisdom that is from above is first pure, then

> **peaceable, gentle, and easy to be intreated, full of mercy and good fruits, without partiality, and without hypocrisy.**
>
> **And the fruit of righteousness is sown in peace of them that make peace.**

At the same time, however, we must be like the dove, who remains at peace and doesn't provoke enmity. God has promised to be our shield and defender if we trust Him to be. The peace and gentleness of God can silence the roar of the enemy if we allow Jesus to be Lord over our emotions and actions in handling difficult people situations.

Thy Gentleness Hath Made Me Great

David the psalmist submitted to the gentle workings of God in his life, which resulted in his success and exaltation. David said, **"...thy *gentleness* hath made me great"** (Psalm 18:35). Had it not been for the gentleness of God, David would not have overcome the failures (adultery, and later, parental failure with his son Absalom) and risen to greatness. David was continually grateful to God for His gentleness toward him. We would all be failures without the gentleness of God in our lives.

In Jeremiah 18:1-6 we read how Jeremiah the prophet was told by the Lord to go to the potter's house and observe the potter. The vessel he made was marred so he made it again. (Note: The potter didn't throw away the marred vessel. Dake explains that "the clay was crushed together and returned to the wheel, and the work begun again."[61] This continued until the clay took the shape the potter intended. This is what God declared He had power to do with Israel.)

"Behold, as the clay is in the potter's hand, so are ye in mine hand, O house of Israel" (Jeremiah 18:6). We who have accepted Jesus Christ as our Lord and Savior are like clay in the potter's hand too. The Potter is God, the Father. His gentle touch in our lives is constantly molding us into a vessel that can be used for His glory.

God works sensitively and gently in our lives, because He knows we are just like a piece of clay. Psalm 103:14 says, **"For he knoweth our frame; he remembereth that we are dust."** God is molding you and me into vessels of honor.

Our flesh often experiences the pressure of this inner working at the hand of God. First Peter 4:1 says, **"Forasmuch then as Christ hath suffered for us in the flesh, arm yourselves likewise with the same mind: for he that hath suffered in the flesh hath ceased from sin."** The more we submit to God's Word and the convictions of the Holy Spirit in our lives, the more our flesh will stop ruling our lives and we will begin walking in the Spirit. Allow your flesh to die so that your life can take on the nature of Jesus. Paul said in 1 Corinthians 15:31, **"...I die daily."** What he meant was that his flesh died daily so that the life of Jesus could operate more and more through his life.

Many newborn Christians still have habits, behavior patterns and sins which God must gently change or remove from their lives by a work of the Holy Spirit. The Holy Spirit will gently change thoughts, desires and habits, conforming the children of God to the image of Christ.

> **And so, as those who have been chosen of God, holy and beloved, put on a heart of compassion, kindness, humility, *gentleness* and patience.**
>
> **Colossians 3:12** NAS

We are to put on *gentleness*, compassion, kindness, humility and patience in the way we treat others, just like we put on clothes each day. We put on the Lord Jesus Christ and make no provision (or opportunity) for the flesh to fulfill its lusts (Romans 13:14). Dake says, "*To be clothed with a person* is a Greek phrase signifying to take upon one the interests of another; to enter into his views; and be wholly on his side, imitating him in all things."[62]

Gentleness is part of the character of Jesus Christ. As we put God's Word in our minds and hearts and seek to exemplify Jesus, we will have His nature flowing through us.

Endotes

[59] Webster, p. 583.
[60] Ibid., p. 443.
[61] Dake, p. 762.
[62] Ibid., p. 171.

CHAPTER 10
GOODNESS

But the fruit of the Spirit is. . . goodness

Galatians 5:22

In the beginning God created the heaven and the earth ... And God saw every thing that he had made, and, behold, it was very good...**" (Genesis 1:1,31). From the beginning, everything God created was good. There was no evil because God is good. His character and nature are good. His plans for man are for good, not for evil (Jeremiah 29:11).

When Moses asked God to show him His glory, God said, **"I will make all my goodness pass before thee, and I will proclaim the name of the Lord before thee ... The Lord God, merciful and gracious, longsuffering, and abundant in *goodness* and *truth*"** (Exodus 33:19; 34:6). God gave Moses a revelation of His character and infinite nature.

Psalm 33:5 says, **"...the earth is full of the goodness of the Lord."** God created the whole earth for the habitation and enjoyment of man. As a good Father He provided the best for His children! Brother Oral Roberts, founder of Oral Roberts University and a world renowned evangelist of salvation and healing, has emphasized for years the fact that "God is a good God."

Many religious leaders have thought God has two natures— good and bad—but He has only one nature and that is good. The devil from the beginning has been evil and has sought to steal, kill and destroy (John 10:10). God has set boundaries for man to live in and principles to live by. Outside of those boundaries which He has revealed to us in His Word, there are penalties. When man chooses to go against those boundaries and principles, he brings upon himself penalties for sin. Sin is the breaking of religious law [God's Word] or moral principle, through a willful act.[63] Sin brings its own judgment. God doesn't desire for man to go through pain and suffering, but man can choose his own way. God's way will bring man toward His goodness. Man's disobedience will bring him toward Satan's destruction.

God's Highest Gift of Goodness to Man

Because God is *so good* He gave the life of His Son Jesus Christ in order to provide a way for man to be cleansed and freed from sin's power and damnation.

> **For God so greatly loved and dearly prized the world that He [even] gave up His only begotten (unique) Son, so that whoever believes in (trusts in, clings to, relies on) Him shall not perish (come to destruction, be lost) but have eternal (everlasting) life.**
>
> **For God did not send the Son into the world in order to judge (to reject, to condemn, to pass sentence on) the world, but that the world might find salvation and be made safe and sound through Him.**
>
> **John 3:16,17** AMP

Through Jesus, we are now able to be restored to God and experience His goodness in our lives. We are able to get back into the good plan He has for us.

People are drawn to God because of His *goodness* and mercy. **"...the goodness of God leadeth thee to repentance"** (Romans 2:4). His love for mankind is exhibited "in spite of," not "because of" what man has done or become. No one but Jesus could love past man's faults and failures. **"But God commendeth his love toward us, in that, while we were yet sinners, Christ died for us"** (Romans 5:8).

"Goodness" Is the Nature of the Father

Another way we know the character of God's goodness is by looking at Jesus. Jesus is the expressed will of God. He said, **"...he that hath seen me hath seen the Father..."** (John 14:9). In reading the four gospels, we can clearly see that Jesus showed us that God's will for us is good. Acts 10:38 says, **"How God anointed Jesus of Nazareth with the Holy Ghost and with power: who went about *doing good*, and *healing* all that were oppressed of the devil; for God was with him."** Jesus said, **"...I am come that they might have life, and that they might have it more abundantly"** (John 10:10).

Some people have been taught that God puts sickness on people or causes tragedy to discipline and teach His children. This does not coincide with Scripture. Jesus never made people sick or caused tragedy. He went about doing good to people and healing those who were sick. Some may say, "Well, what about the Old Testament incidents of sickness and judgment?" Again, remember, God did not intend evil for mankind in the beginning. Mankind chose to sin and sin brought its own judgment or penalty. Those who turned to God received mercy.

God teaches and disciplines us with His Word and His Spirit. The psalmist David said, **"...thy rod** [His Word] **and thy staff** [His Spirit] **they comfort me"** (Psalm 23:4). The rod is an instrument of discipline and the staff is an instrument of guidance or direction. The shepherd uses the rod to get the sheep away from the wrong path that could destroy them, and the staff is used to guide and instruct them to go another direction. If we choose the wrong path, circumstances can be very humbling and can create an opportunity to learn a lesson. But again, it depends upon whether or not man chooses to allow God to teach him. Otherwise, he may continue to stay on the wrong path and slowly or quickly face destruction.

God our Father offers discipline in the highest form of love. He said, **"All scripture is given by inspiration of God, and is profitable...for *reproof*, for *correction*, for *instruction* in**

righteousness" (2 Timothy 3:16). Not only do we receive reproof and correction through the Word of God, but we also receive instruction and inspiration to build us up.

How many times have you, as a Christian, felt the correction of God's Word when you read it or heard it preached and immediately you wanted to make a change and correct your ways? I have felt His correction many times.

Now that we've established God's character of goodness, realize that He has come to live within you and His nature and goodness are now yours. Ephesians 5:9,10 says, **"For the fruit of the Spirit is in all goodness and righteousness and truth; proving what is acceptable unto the Lord."** We are now to be imitators of God our Father as dear children. In the natural, children imitate their parents. We're to imitate God—to want to be like Him and do what we've seen Jesus do in the Word.

The Fruit of Goodness in Your Life— Like Father, Like Child

Agathosune is the Greek word for *goodness* in the Scriptures. It means "the state of being good, kind, benevolent, generous, and God-like in life and conduct."[64] God says we're to be imitators of Him. When we are born again and Jesus comes to make His home in us, we receive His fruit of goodness. Like the other fruit at this stage, it is only a seed and must be nourished with the Word of God to grow and produce in our lives. No longer are we trying to work at being good by our own ability, but instead, we begin to allow the nature of Christ to mature in us and flow out from us!

What does this mean practically speaking? Matthew 5:44-48 tells us we are to love our enemies, bless them who curse us, do good to them who hate us and pray for them who despitefully use us and persecute us that we may be children of our Father Who is in heaven. He concludes these verses with, **"Be ye therefore perfect, even as your Father which is in heaven is perfect"** (v.

48). The word *perfect* as used in this verse is *teleios* in the Greek and means complete in conformity to God's laws.[65]

I realize that no person is without sin. Only Jesus is perfect and without sin. However, Paul says in Philippians 3:15, **"Let us therefore, as many as be perfect, be thus minded…."** Paul had just spoken about forgetting those things which are behind and reaching forth unto those things which are before and pressing (or making every effort) toward the mark for the prize of the high calling of God in Christ Jesus. Here in Philippians 3:15, the word *perfect* means mature, complete, full grown in the knowledge of God and His Word; thoroughly instructed and deeply experienced in living for Jesus. It takes a conscious choice to mature spiritually. It is in making choices to think and act according to the Word of God on a daily basis.

Goodness in a person will cause him or her to love and not hate, to bless when others curse, to do good and pray for those who treat them wrongly. This is totally against the desires of the flesh. The flesh always feels justified to act in its own way, but Jesus tells us that the character of God is just the opposite.

Luke 6:27-35 goes on to say that if someone slaps you on one cheek, offer him the other cheek to slap also. If someone takes your coat, go ahead and give it from your heart so you don't allow bitterness. Give to every man what he asks of you, and if someone takes what belongs to you, don't ask for it back. Let God handle it. Your reward for doing good, loving your enemies and giving will be great and you'll be known as children of the Highest. God will bring back to you everything you sow as a seed if you believe for Him to turn things for good.

When Billy Joe and I have made a decision to release anything that had already been taken from us, and not hold a grudge, God has restored to us and blessed us with other things over and over again. We've also seen that when we've done good to others who hated us, many times it has been the very thing that has caused them to change their way of thinking toward us.

I heard about a minister who attacked another minister

publicly. The offended minister attacked back. Later, however, the offended minister felt badly for striking back, publicly apologized and invited the offending minister to his church. This minister accepted his apology and invitation. When he came to the church of the man he had attacked, he saw that he was a very sincere minister of the Gospel, so he also apologized and reconciled with the minister. Jesus is looking for and calling for fruit that everyone can see.

Just Doing Good Works
Will Not Get You into Heaven

As we talk about good works, it is important to realize that you are not saved by your own good works, but by faith in Jesus. However, good works should accompany the salvation experience. One religion teaches that it is by our good works that we get into heaven. However, it is by faith in the cleansing blood of Jesus that we get into heaven, as we believe and confess Him as Lord. Our good works are to be the fruit of our salvation, not the basis of it.

The good works actually are working out (carrying out) your salvation—becoming a *doer of the Word* that has been heard and received. **"Wherefore, my beloved, as ye have always obeyed, not as in my presence only, but now much more in my absence, *work out* [cultivate, carry out to the goal and fully complete] your own salvation with fear and trembling. For it is God which worketh in you both to will and to do of his good pleasure"** (Philippians 2:12,13).

Ephesians 2:10 says, **"For we are his workmanship, created in Christ Jesus unto good works, which God hath before ordained that we should walk in them."** Before the foundation of the world, God had you and me in mind, as well as all mankind who would live on the earth. He also has a plan for us to walk in that which is characterized by good works. Whatever He asks you to do will be good.

In Luke 6:43-45, Jesus says that *a good tree brings forth good fruit,* and a corrupt tree brings forth corrupt fruit. He goes on to say that every tree is known by its fruit. The good works which accompany your salvation are a reflection of the life of Christ within you.

Do You Have a Zeal for Goodness?

Jesus redeemed you that you might be a peculiar people, zealous of good works. **"Who gave himself for us, that he might redeem us from all iniquity, and purify unto himself a peculiar people, *zealous of good works*"** (Titus 2:14). Are you zealous of good works? God has called you to be.

Dorcas was a woman "full of good works." She oversaw the ministry of women to the poor. When she died prematurely, her life was so needed that they sent for Peter to raise her from the dead, and she was raised up to continue in the ministry gift with which she was anointed. Acts 11:24 says Barnabas **"...was a *good* man, and full of the Holy Ghost and of faith ....."**

Hebrews 10:24 says we should provoke [urge] one another **"unto love and to good works."** I believe Barnabas' example of mentoring young Christian men was provoking to the other disciples to mentor young men in the Lord. The Scripture is full of examples of men and women who consecrated themselves unto the Lord for good works. The natural flow of the fruit of goodness was abundant in their lives.

Paul admonishes Christians to follow that which is good. **"See that none render evil for evil unto any man; but ever follow that which is good, both among yourselves, and to all men"** (1 Thessalonians 5:15). Matthew 5:16 also says, **"Let your light so shine before men, that they may see your good works, and glorify your Father which is in heaven."** Your Christian lifestyle should so exhibit the character of Christ that all men will be drawn unto Him. Your light should be consistent in the words you speak and in the life you live.

Paul prayed that the church of Colosse "**...might walk worthy of the Lord unto all pleasing, being fruitful in every good work, and increasing in the knowledge of God**" (Colossians 1:10). As we increase in the knowledge of God, we will increase in His nature and in how we relate to others.

Salt That Is Good and Salt That Is Good for Nothing

The scripture says in Matthew 5:13 that you and I are the salt of the earth and that salt is good, "**...but if the salt have lost his savour, wherewith shall it be salted? it is thenceforth good for nothing....**"

Some characteristics of salt are as follows. Salt is found everywhere—in animals, in vegetables, in minerals, in caves and in the ocean. And so it is with Christians—they can be found everywhere, even in remote areas. People are being saved in every walk of life, and the presence of these born-again people is as salt. Salt acts as a preservative. The Christian's presence in the earth is the preserving factor to keep the forces of evil (decay) from bringing total destruction upon the earth.

Salt makes people thirsty. As a Christian, your presence should make people thirsty for God! When you are around a non-Christian and he sees how blessed you are and how effectively you are able to deal with life's problems, he will desire what you have. Check yourself. Are you walking in peace with people? Is there joy in your life? Are you keeping your heart pure? Are you loving others unconditionally? Are you a giving person? Are you affecting people around you in a good or positive way?

If you are conscious of living honorably among unsaved people—even if they are suspicious of you or talk against you— they will end up praising God for your good works. "**Having your conversation honest among the Gentiles: that, whereas they** speak against you as evildoers, they may by your good works, which they shall behold, glorify God in the day of visitation" (1 Peter 2:12).

Salt is a healing agent. *You* are God's healing agent in the earth because of the Holy Spirit residing within you. Your words are to be words of healing to those around you. The Word of God within you has the power to set at liberty those who are bruised and deliver those who are held captive. Some people need an inner healing; others need physical healing. God has given His Word and His Spirit so you can minister to all kinds of people in all kinds of situations. God has no alternative but to use people—you and me—as channels of His goodness, His love and His power in this earth.

Just as salt will melt ice, God will use your life and the warmth of your words to melt the coldness and hardness of people's hearts. You'll reflect the warmth of God's love and others will be convicted. Walls will begin to come down as believers move in the compassion of Jesus.

You are the salt of the earth, but if salt has lost its taste (its strength, its quality), how can its saltness be restored? It is not good for anything any longer but to be thrown out and trodden underfoot by men.

Matthew 5:13 AMP

Salt which has lost its flavor is fit for nothing, not even for fertilizer. It is thrown out, and men trample it underfoot. Some who have lost the fervor of God's Spirit have been trampled underfoot by people in this world. But if you have lost your fervor and flavoring, unlike the salt, you can become full of flavor again if you seek God. Do not allow slothfulness or the cares of this life to rob you of your usefulness (of the salt in you). Instead, keep the zeal of God. It will motivate you to press after Him to be conformed more and more into His image (Philippians 3:13-15; 2 Corinthians 3:18).

God's goodness is in you. His power is within you. You have all you need through the Word for you to live the Christian life.

God shows us in Micah 6:8 ᴀᴍᴘ how to walk in His goodness. **"He has showed you, O man, *what is good.* And what does the Lord require of you but *to do justly* [or to do what is right], and *to love kindness and mercy, and to humble yourself and walk humbly with your God?"***

When you're walking right, there is a confidence in God that no matter what is happening around you, God will work all things together for good. When you are a merciful person toward others, you'll receive mercy, and when you keep a humble attitude about you, others will enjoy being around you. James 4:6 says, **"...God resisteth the proud, but giveth grace unto the humble."** God favors those who are humble.

God surrounds His children with His favor, His goodness and His mercy as we surrender our lives to Him and choose to walk in His ways of goodness. **"Surely goodness and mercy shall follow me all the days of my life..."** (Psalm 23:6).

Endotes

[63] Webster, p. 1328.
[64] Vine, p. 495.
[65] Dake, pp. 5, 217.

CHAPTER 11
FAITHFULNESS

But the fruit of the Spirit is. . . faithfulness.

Galatians 5:22 NIV

Webster defines *faithful* as maintaining an allegiance to someone or something; to be constant; loyal; having or showing a strong sense of duty or responsibility; conscientious. *Faithful* also implies continued, steadfast adherence to a person or thing to which one is bound by an oath, duty, or obligation (such as in marriage). *Loyal* implies having an undeviating allegiance to a person, cause, or institution which one feels morally bound to support or defend. *Constant* suggests freedom from fickleness in affections or loyalties.

The opposite of faithful would imply failure to adhere to an oath, duty, or obligation; failure in devotion to someone or something that has a moral claim to one's support; not keeping faith; being dishonest; disloyal; unreliable and undependable.[66] God is faithful. He keeps His Word. He is constant and unchanging.

It is because of the Lord's mercy and loving-kindness that we are not consumed, because His [tender] compassions fail not.

They are new every morning; great and abundant is Your stability and *faithfulness*.

Lamentations 3:22,23 AMP

God is always faithful to keep His covenant with men. Even when men are not faithful, God remains faithful to His Word. Second Timothy 2:13 says even **"if we believe not, yet he abideth faithful: he cannot deny himself."** God's Word is forever settled

113

in heaven and stands fast without change. God's faithfulness to keep His Word is to all generations (Psalm 119:89,90).

Numbers 23:19 NIV says:

God is not a man, that he should lie, nor a son of man, that he should change his mind. Does he speak and then not act? Does he promise and not fulfill?

In Psalm 89:34 God says, **"My covenant will I not break, nor alter the thing that is gone out of my lips."** The Old Covenant, or better known to Christians as the Old Testament, was God's Word given to Abraham and his seed of the Jewish race. Jesus came with the New Covenant, the New Testament, based upon His blood sacrifice. It is a new and better covenant, established upon better promises (Hebrews 8:6). Our belief and faith in Jesus cause us to enter into all the promises of God's Word, both in the Old and New Covenant. (See Hebrews, chapters 8 and 9; Galatians 3:7-9,13,14,26-29.) God's Word is His covenant to us. **"He is faithful that promised"** (Hebrews 10:23). We can believe God and His Word. He and His Word are one. He keeps His Word. Faithfulness will cause us to keep our word, which is integrity—doing what we say we will do.

Today in our society many people lack faithfulness and integrity and do not keep their word. This creates distrust, disappointment, hurt and suffering in others. It also causes others not to believe in them or become involved with them financially, maritally, etc. because they don't want to experience loss and hurt again. Psalm 15:4 says a righteous man (or woman) will swear to his or her own hurt and not change. *The New International Version* of this verse says, **"...**[he or she] **keeps his** [or her] **oath** [his or her word of commitment] **even when it hurts."**

Anyone who has the Spirit of God inside of them will be dealt with to keep their word. This is God's nature and character. Those who do not keep their word have shut out God's Spirit and have hardened their hearts to His voice. (See Hebrews 3:7-13).

Over the years I've observed whenever it has been difficult momentarily to go ahead and fulfill our commitment to others, it has later produced a harvest of good in our lives. I've also observed when people have established a lifestyle of only keeping their word when it's convenient or comfortable and not keeping promises when it is hard, that they reap a harvest of suffering later on.

Proverbs 28:20 says, **"A faithful man shall abound with blessings."** The seeds we sow today toward walking in good character will come back to us in blessings, but if we sow seeds toward lack of character, it will come back to us in time with the curse. (See Deuteronomy 28—the blessings and the curses.) Proverbs 26:2 says, **"...the curse causeless shall not come."**

The curse is not just a momentary difficulty or tragedy. The curse lingers with bad circumstances. I have watched some people who have had one bad thing after another happen to them that robs, shames, destroys, or kills and they've wondered why. Sometimes it is caused by breaking promises in life that they never reconciled.

God's faithfulness is revealed to us time and time again through His relationship with the children of Israel. Although the children of Israel rejected God many times, He always remained loyal to His covenant with them. Every time they called to Him, He displayed His faithfulness in power and greatness. He continually delivered them from their sin and their enemies. He had entered into covenant with Abraham and He had to keep His promises. The relationship between God and Abraham was total commitment and it was to Abraham's seed.

As born-again believers, we have a covenant with God through Jesus Christ our Mediator. We become the seed of Abraham through faith in Jesus Christ. It is a covenant of total commitment. Just like Abraham, when we give God our all, He promises to give us all we need in this life and an eternal home. He keeps His promises to those who believe because faithfulness is His character. First Corinthians 1:9 says, **"God is faithful, by whom ye were called unto the fellowship of his Son Jesus Christ our Lord."** If we sin or fail to keep our part of the covenant, He promises if we confess (repent and turn from our sins), God will forgive and restore our fellowship with Him.

If we [freely] admit that we have sinned and confess our sins, He is faithful and just (true to His own nature and promises) and will forgive our sins [dismiss our lawlessness] and [continuously] cleanse us from all unrighteousness [everything not in conformity to His will in purpose, thought, and action].

1 John 1:9 AMP

It is through the blood of Jesus that we are cleansed and reconciled back to God, for Hebrews 2:17 says that Jesus is a *faithful*, merciful High Priest, standing in the gap, always interceding to God for us.

Jesus' Example of Faithfulness

Jesus was faithful, even to the point of death. Looking at the faithfulness of Jesus to God our Father, we see that faithfulness sometimes must go beyond personal feelings. Many times faithfulness requires the sacrifice of self.

Wherefore in all things it behoved him to be made like unto his brethren, that he might be a merciful and *faithful* high priest in things pertaining to God, to make reconciliation for the sins of the people.

For in that he himself hath suffered being tempted, he is able to succour them that are tempted.

Wherefore, holy brethren, partakers of the heavenly calling, consider the Apostle and High Priest of our profession, Christ Jesus;

Who was faithful to him that appointed him....

Hebrews 2:17,18; 3:1,2

Jesus had to remain faithful to His Father's will by going through the cross experience, suffering the agony of it to provide salvation for us. He died and was resurrected that we might be made the righteousness of God in Christ (2 Corinthians 5:21). The Scripture says in Hebrews 12 that Jesus endured the cross for the joy that was set before Him. Jesus had to press beyond His momentary feeling to a greater joy of reward. He could rejoice, knowing that many would come into the Kingdom because of His obedience.

Luke 9:23 says, **"And he said to them all, If any man will come after me, let him deny himself, and take up his cross daily, and follow me."** Faithfulness often requires the denial of self to do what will benefit others. The cross can simply be defined as "doing God's will." In order to do God's will and continue to do it, you must move in faithfulness and firm commitment. Often, self-denial is involved in walking out this fruit.

Over the years I've watched people who have volunteered to serve in the ministry be promoted by God to staff positions because of their faithfulness and willingness to sacrifice in different ways. They went the "extra mile" when they were not asked to. They completed a job when they could have gone home. They didn't criticize or mock those who were over them. They did what they were doing as unto the Lord and God rewarded them. (See Colossians 3:23-25.) (Note: This happens in the realm of business also. Faithful people get promotions, increases and positions that others don't get.)

Let the Fruit of Faithfulness Mature in You

There are times when God will prove your faithfulness. Often, He will place you in seemingly unimportant positions, all the while observing your faithfulness in the little things. God will not promote a person who is unfaithful (irresponsible) in the little things. Faithful people feel responsible for the things they do and the people they serve. They do not quit because they are tired, offended, or because there is inconvenience. They go on to complete tasks they've been given.

People who are undependable or irresponsible will not be given leadership positions. A leader must be responsible and faithful. Proverbs 25:19 says, **"Confidence in an unfaithful man in time**

117

of trouble is like a broken tooth, and a foot out of joint." People who are not dependable or faithful can be a pain to those who work or live with them.

Daniel's Faithfulness

Let's take a look at Daniel. In Daniel 6:1-4 we see that Daniel had been promoted to the level of being a first president under King Darius. He had already proven faithful through the reign of two previous kings. Darius, however, had promoted him because he valued Daniel's wisdom and character above all the other men around him. This caused jealousy in others who wanted his position. They began to look for ways to trap him but could not find character flaws. Daniel 6:4 says, **"... but they could find none occasion nor fault; forasmuch as he was *faithful*, neither was there any error or fault found in him."** Daniel was faithful to God and to his king. (Note: Those who are faithful to God will show faithfulness to those who are in authority over them.)

Daniel's enemies had to resort to deception in order to trap him in his faithfulness to pray daily. Although Daniel ended up in the lions' den because of doing what was right, God protected him by shutting the lions' mouths. After the king retrieved him unharmed, the king put the deceivers into the same lions' den and they were eaten.

Faithfulness does not always mean circumstances will be favorable, but as you are willing to walk out your commitment to God and to your assignment, God will deliver you and promote you. We must learn how to stand steadfast and immovable in what we know is right.

Three Men's Response to Responsibility and Gifts

Let's observe the characteristics of the three men in Matthew, chapter 25, regarding the parable of the talents. Two of the men who worked for the master were faithful with what was entrusted to their responsibility. When the master returned, he made the same statement to both of these men:

. . .Well done, you upright (honorable, admirable) and faithful servant! You have been faithful and trustworthy over a little; I will put you in charge of much. Enter into and share the joy (the delight, the blessedness) which your master enjoys.

Matthew 25:21,23 AMP

A faithful servant will always be trusted to handle his responsibilities wisely, to the best of his ability. A faithful servant is always dependable. When given a task, he will complete it. He deals honestly in the affairs of life. When he sees something that needs to be done, he is willing to go beyond what is expected of him to do it. And finally, the person who is faithful is the one who enters into the joy of the Lord.

The reward of the good and faithful servant was added responsibility as well as the privilege of entering into the joy of the Lord. There is joy in obedience. God can bless and promote you when you are faithful.

I give thanks to Him Who has granted me [the needed] strength and made me able [for this], Christ Jesus our Lord, because He has judged and counted me faithful and trustworthy, appointing me to [this stewardship of] the ministry.

1 Timothy 1:12 AMP

Paul said he gave thanks and rejoiced in knowing that God had considered him faithful and that he had been appointed to the leadership ministry position that he was in. To you who desire a greater ministry, God is saying, "be faithful where you are, and i will advance you in due time, and with that advancement will be added responsibility."

So then, let us [apostles] be looked upon as ministering servants of Christ and stewards (trustees) of the mysteries (the secret purposes) of God.

Moreover, it is [essentially] required of stewards

119

that a man should be found faithful [proving himself worthy of trust].

1 Corinthians 4:1,2 AMP

Be faithful to your time in the Word and in prayer. Be faithful to serve wherever you are asked if it is within your ability to serve at the time. Be faithful to be a hard worker. Do your duties with a desire for excellence (not sloppy or halfhearted). Be willing to stretch yourself in order to obey God.

One of the servants in Matthew 25 was found unfaithful. Three characteristics of the unfaithful servant, typical of some of God's people today, are brought out in *Dake's Reference Bible.*

1. He accuses his master in order to excuse his own slothfulness.[67] His accusation was not true, however. If the master had indeed reaped where he had not sown, he would not have been a man of great wealth. He had to sow in order to reap. The servant's attempt to shift the blame to his master merely reveals his own attitude of laziness and insecurity. Some people today are a lot of talk but manifest no fruit. They are quick to criticize or blame their circumstances, their past, their heredity, the government, or whoever they can for their lack of finances, position, or their lack of recognition.

2. The slothful person thinks that everything others do prospers and that he is just not lucky.[68] Many times he is failure-conscious. He usually thinks other people just happen to know the right people. Don't let the enemy trick you with this kind of thinking! Joshua 1:8 AMP tells us what a man must do if he expects to prosper:

This Book of the Law *shall not depart out of your mouth*, but you shall *meditate* on it day and night, that you may *observe and do* according to all that is written in it. For then you shall make your way prosperous, and then you shall deal wisely and have good success.

3. A slothful person is always afraid to venture out in business or take risks.[69] He is afraid to step out in faith. However, a faithful person will step out as God reveals things to him, trusting that

God will bring to pass those things He has made known to him. Sometimes God might expect you to step out further than you can clearly see, but He will always uphold you.

The Spirit of God will always encourage you to take bigger steps of faith. That's the way to let the fruit of faithfulness (as well as all of the other fruit) mature in you.

Many people have tremendous potential, but they have not been faithful. Sometimes a faithful person who isn't necessarily the most talented will be promoted over a highly talented person simply because of faithfulness. It's the same way within a ministry. People sometimes wonder why they haven't been promoted into advanced positions as quickly as others, but my first question would be, "Have they been faithful? Have they fulfilled the tasks they have been given, even though they may seem like small tasks?"

My husband was a janitor as a teenager, then a volunteer coach, an assistant at a boys' club, a youth pastor and then we traveled in ministry over a season of three years to small churches that could not afford to have evangelists come and preach. In those churches we simply received whatever was given to us. Following this time period we began pastoring. As time has progressed, our lives have taken on more responsibility.

God Can Take an Unfaithful Person and Make Him Faithful

God can change an unfaithful person. He can transform him into a faithful person through the power of the Holy Spirit. When a person recognizes his sin and turns to God to change him, He will. For example, even though Peter was unfaithful to Jesus and denied Him three times, it was evident he had become a different man by the Day of Pentecost. He had become faithful to God, faithful to what God had called him to do, and faithful to proclaim with boldness God's Word everywhere he went.

The power of the Holy Spirit can help produce within a person the willingness and the grace to be faithful, even in a person who has previously been unfaithful. I've watched God work miraculously in marriages where one spouse was unfaithful and turn that spouse around to be stronger in their love for God and for their mate than before, when they repented and received help.

God is calling His people to commitment and to faithfulness. Over the years, particularly in Charismatic/Pentecostal churches, some people have hopped from one church to another, "skimming the cream off the milk," so to speak. There is nothing wrong with visiting different churches occasionally, but God wants to get His people past the "floating around" stage into a stable commitment to one church body so they can grow and mature to their maximum potential.

Psalm 92:13,14 says:

Those that be planted in the house of the Lord shall flourish in the courts of our God. They shall still bring forth fruit in old age....

Get planted in a church. Don't be a tumbleweed tossed around by every wind of doctrine or adversity. God can stabilize you.

We must grow beyond the "I don't want to get tied down" syndrome if we expect to grow and bear fruit. My husband has said that people need to hear from God where they are assigned and be planted there. He shared how soldiers go where they are assigned. Pigs go where they are fed. Are you a soldier or a pig? Possibly you are a soldier who has gone awol – away without "official" leave. If so, get back quickly and be restored to the church God has called you to. Don't let offenses separate you. That's how Satan is deceiving and destroying some Christians. It's time to grow up. Learn how to forgive like Jesus and become faithful. If you uproot a plant and replant it every few months or every year, you'll dwarf or stunt its growth.

In committing to one church body, it is like drinking whole milk. A steady diet of skimming the cream will not allow for proper growth. God has provided for your overall development through the establishment of the local church, but commitment requiring involvement and faithfulness is essential. Sometimes a person's faithfulness to a local church body will determine the effectiveness of the entire Body of Christ. My dad used to say, "If everyone in this church was just like me, what kind of a church would this church be?"

Are you faithful in your attendance, your tithes, your abilities, your prayers, and in the time given to the work of the Lord? What an impact the church would have on a community—and even the world—if all its members were found faithful!

John F. Kennedy once said, "Ask not what your country can do for you, but ask what you can do for your country." As Christians we could say, "Ask not what your church can do for you, ask what you can do for your church." Those who give their lives in some way to serve faithfully are more committed and stable Christians than those who are simply consumers within the church. Let the grace of God help you grow in faithfulness.

Keys for Being Faithful

Some helpful hints for being faithful are:

1. Keep your word.

2. Do all you can do to the best of your ability in the assignment you are in.

3. Do what you are assigned to do, whether others see you or not. God sees you!

4. Go the extra mile if it is necessary in order to complete an assigned task.

5. Maintain a sense of responsibility, realizing that others may be depending upon the part you do. Remove from your thinking the attitude that someone else will do it.

6. Stay put when others jump out at the first difficulty. Learn to stay until you've spent time and heard direction from God before considering a move.

7. Keep a good attitude and avoid listening to scorners.

8. Submit to authority and learn to follow. Then God can promote you more quickly to a leadership position.

9. Don't look for changes to always happen in others around you. Instead, learn to look inside yourself and allow God to change you even more into His character.

Rewards of Faithfulness

There are rewards for the faithful servant, too!

1. **"A faithful man shall abound with blessings. . ."** (Proverbs 28:20).

2. **"O love the Lord, all ye his saints: for the Lord preserveth the faithful"** (Psalm 31:23).

3. **". . .thou hast been faithful over a few things, I will make thee ruler over many things..."** (Matthew 25:21).

4. **". . .he counted me faithful, putting me into the ministry"** (1 Timothy 1:12).

5. **". . .be thou faithful unto death, and I will give thee a crown of life"** (Revelation 2:10).

Endotes

66 Webster, p. 503.
67 Dake, p. 28.
68 Ibid.
69 Ibid.

CHAPTER 12
MEEKNESS

But the fruit of the Spirit is. . . meekness

Galatians 5:22,23

*M*eekness in the Greek is *praotes*, meaning the disposition to be gentle, kind, indulgent, even balanced in tempers and passions, and patient in suffering injuries without feeling a spirit of revenge.[70]

W. E. Vine defines *praotes* or *prautes* as denoting meekness. It does not consist of a person's outward behavior only.... It is an inwrought grace of the soul toward God. It is that temper of spirit in which we accept His dealings with us as good, and therefore without disputing or resisting. It is first of all a meekness before God and is also such in the face of men, even of evil men, out of a sense that these, with the insults and injuries which they may inflict, are permitted and employed by Him for the chastening and purifying of His elect. *Prautes* describes a condition of mind and heart, and gentleness is appropriate rather to actions. Some have thought meekness is weakness, but the Lord displayed meekness and He had all the power He needed had He wanted to retaliate or resist, but He chose not to. Meekness is the fruit of power. It is the opposite of self-assertiveness and self-interest. It is not occupied with self at all but with what can benefit others.[71]

Another definition of meekness for us as Christians is "to be totally dependent upon God." Without Him, we can do nothing. We know that the talents and wisdom we've acquired must still have God's anointing; otherwise it is simply empty speeches or performances. A person of humility realizes that he is what he is

125

because of God, not because of anything else.

Moses: An Example of Excellence in the Fruit of Meekness

Let's take a look at Moses, the man whom the Bible called the meekest man on the face of the earth (Numbers 12:3). Moses had been brought up in Pharaoh's household and received the best in education and training. When he realized the call God had placed upon him to deliver His people Israel from the Egyptian oppression, Moses tried to deliver them in his own ability.

Sometimes when people receive a call of God, they try to make it happen in their own efforts and natural talent. Moses relied first upon his natural training, but after failure he ran to escape, thinking he could do something else. In this time period, he made a decision to forget all of his educational accomplishments and leadership training in the house of Pharaoh and was humbly grateful for tending sheep. This position of humility was exactly where God wanted him so he would look totally to Him. When God called Moses to return and deliver His people, Moses would only go as long as he knew God was in each step.

Some have missed God's highest plan because they have started out relying upon their own natural talents and training. Some have failed and given up, because they didn't wait upon the Lord for His timing and anointing for the task. Some continue to strive all of their lives, trying to make something happen and it never really happens. Usually, these people feel that those who do succeed in their calling are just lucky or favored more than they are. If they would only stop striving, search their own souls, release it to God and become content and thankful, they would find peace, fulfillment and God's divine intervention in their lives.

After Moses failed to free the people because he relied on his own strength, he fled into the wilderness, but he could not escape the call of God. No one is truly able to escape the call of God that is upon his or her life. God came to Moses in this place and let him know He still wanted to use him to deliver His people. It was in this position of humility and total dependence upon God that Moses returned to carry out his calling.

God will not throw away your talents, education, or training, but He will bring you to a place of *total dependence upon Him* rather than letting you depend upon your own abilities. He will allow you to see that it is not by your might or power, talent or looks, or who you know, but by His Spirit that you achieve success in obeying whatever He says (Zechariah 4:6).

Second Corinthians 3:5,6 NLT says:

It is not that we think we can do anything of lasting value by ourselves. Our only power and success come from God. He is the one who has enabled us to represent his new covenant. This is a covenant, not of written laws, but of the Spirit. The old way ends in death; in the new way, the Holy Spirit gives life.

You will notice that Moses kept an attitude of meekness even after becoming a successful leader. He realized he had to remain totally dependent upon God and submitted to Him.

In Numbers 12:2, Miriam and Aaron challenged Moses being the only one who heard from God, saying, **"Hath the Lord indeed spoken only by Moses? hath he not spoken also by us? And the Lord heard it."** Note how Moses didn't try to defend himself, he let God do it for him and God did. Miriam got leprosy because of her pride and contentious attitude. Her sin opened the door to her sickness. Aaron asked Moses to pray for Miriam. Seven days later she was healed and restored. That took meekness and compassion to pray for restoration for the one who had come against him.

Although Aaron and Miriam were older than Moses and were his brother and sister, they had to realize that Moses was the one God had anointed to lead. They learned the importance of submission to God-given authority.

Many people don't want to submit to others because they are not submitted to the authority – God's authority. We first must be submitted to God. (Note: If you are truly submitted to God, you are also submitted to His Word. Submission to God's Word includes submission to natural authorities such as governmental laws *that are not against God's Word*, government officials, church pastors, elders, employers and authority within the home.)

Submission is a word which has been widely misunderstood. It actually means "yielded obedience." It should be our goal to yield to and obey God and those in authority over us. The flesh will suffer at times, but that is for our good. If you are submitted to God, you will submit to others who are in leadership around you. (I will reiterate that the submission is not in regard to sin or physical endangerment.)

You can learn spiritual lessons in submission within the natural realm, at home, at school, or at your place of employment. Learn to submit to those in authority over you. Children who are raised to submit to their parents will submit to an employer more quickly. It will also be easier for them to submit to God as they grow into adulthood. When any person strives to submit to God, he will be more submissive to earthly authorities. God cannot use you extensively until you learn to be submissive to His commands and to His will.

Through the years I've met Christians who felt called into ministry who had grandiose visions but weren't willing to plant themselves somewhere and submit to learn under others' authority. Many have been wanderers – wandering from one conference or campmeeting to another, never bringing forth much fruit, tossed to and fro.

God's call to leadership will not be without difficulty. Those who are called by God will stand in the midst of difficulty and lead responsibly through it.

Moses faced not only physical obstacles (such as the Red Sea), but he had to deal with constant murmuring and complaining from his people. There will be critical and complaining people. However, the meek will simply go on and do what they're called to do and leave their defense with God. A leading evangelist once said, "While the dogs bark, the train rolls on by." Meekness will cause a person to be forbearing with antagonizing people. A person operating in meekness will allow God to handle matters rather than retaliate in the flesh.

The Scripture says *the Lord Himself spoke from heaven* commanding Moses, Miriam and Aaron to come into the tabernacle. God then appeared in a pillar of cloud, and His anger was kindled against Miriam and Aaron. God required Miriam to remain outside the camp for seven days before she became totally clean of leprosy. This was time enough to think about what she had done in speaking against God's anointed. I would imagine that she watched her words and attitude after this experience. Sometimes people go through difficult illnesses before they realize their own words and attitudes have been an open door for the enemy to come into their life.

The Word of God says, **"...Touch not mine anointed, and do my prophets no harm"** (1 Chronicles 16:22). Be cautious about speaking against brothers and sisters in Christ and against God's ministers, no matter what you think is wrong or what you see wrong. Instead of criticizing, murmuring and complaining, immediately go to prayer in their behalf, and if you can speak to them, then go to them personally in a spirit of meekness. Prayer still changes things! Prayer will change you, and it will also change people and circumstances.

Time and time again, Moses interceded for the people, even though they still murmured against him. It takes great strength of character and tremendous forbearance to do that.

Along with the privilege of being a leader, Moses shouldered the massive responsibility of an entire nation. With the privileges of leadership come great responsibilities.

If you are ever placed in a position of leadership, there will be times when you will have to be forbearing with others, regardless of their actions toward you. If a leader does not walk in the spirit of meekness and forbearance, eventually he may find himself relieved of his position of leadership and authority.

The opposite of meekness is pride. Obadiah, verse 3, says,

"**The pride of thine heart hath deceived thee. . . .**" Those who are proud are self-deceived. They feel that they know better than others. Therefore, it is difficult for them to receive instruction or correction from others. Usually, they feel they are right and others are wrong. It is difficult for them to take a servant position because they feel they are "above" that position.

Obadiah, verse 4, goes on to say, "**Though thou exalt thyself as the eagle, and though thou set thy nest among the stars, thence will I bring thee down, saith the Lord.**" Proverbs 29:23 says, "**A man's pride shall bring him low: but honour shall uphold the humble in spirit.**" God will uphold those who humble themselves. No matter what test you face, He will take you through and honor you in the end.

A prideful person is also contentious. Proverbs 13:10 says, "**Only *by pride cometh contention*: but with the well advised is wisdom.**" The proud also speak foolishly and it causes their downfall (Proverbs 14:3). Satan's downfall was his pride (Isaiah 14:12-15; Ezekiel 28:11-17; Luke 10:18). The humble person will guard his mouth from speaking too quickly and will listen to others' advice. "**But the wisdom that is from above is first pure, then peaceable, gentle, and easy to be intreated, full of mercy and good fruits, without partiality, and without hypocrisy**" (James 3:17).

Have the Mind of Christ

Let's look at the attitude of Jesus:

Let this mind be in you, which was also in Christ Jesus:

Who, being in the form of God, thought it not robbery to be equal with God:

But made himself of no reputation, and took upon him the form of a servant, and was made in the likeness of men:

And being found in fashion as a man, he humbled

himself, and became obedient unto death, even the death of the cross.

Wherefore God also hath highly exalted him, and given him a name which is above every name:

That at the name of Jesus every knee should bow, of things in heaven, and things in earth, and things under the earth;

And that every tongue should confess that Jesus Christ is Lord, to the glory of God the Father.

Philippians 2:5-11

First of all, although He was the Son of God and in the highest position, Jesus made Himself of no reputation and took upon Himself the form of a servant. Most people today are trying to make themselves a reputation and rise to the top quickly. Rather than be content to serve wherever they can, they want to serve only where it will benefit them to be seen and promoted. If it doesn't benefit them for promotion or to be noticed, then they look for other places to rise to the top.

Jesus' attitude was to serve. Even though He was a leader, He never wore His title as a badge. Many today seek titles in front of their name. Jesus' title was His name – "Jesus Christ." He was apostle, prophet, pastor, evangelist, teacher, healer, Savior and all that we need.

I've known of people who had several degrees and titles by their name but not many people wanted to listen to them speak. I've known of others with no degrees or titles who had masses come to hear them speak. The difference was the compassion and simplicity of the Gospel message that was spoken.

Secondly, Jesus took the form of a servant. Matthew 20:20-28 tells us the incident of James and John's mother coming to Jesus desiring a certain position for her two sons. In her carnal mind, she had no idea that the honored position she was desiring for her sons was to be determined at death by the Father God. Jesus explained that in the Kingdom of God, whoever desired to be great or chief among others would have to become a servant to others. He went on to say that He, the Son of man (and the Son of God), came not to be served but to serve and to give His life a ransom for many as a payment price for man, to buy man back.

Those who desire to lead or have a position will find, like Paul, that they will have to die daily (1 Corinthians 15:31). It is a death to the flesh. Romans 8:13 says, **"For if ye live after the flesh, ye shall die: but if ye through the Spirit do mortify the deeds of the body, ye shall live."** *Frustrated Christians are those who've not learned to let the flesh die and live by the Spirit.*

It does not matter whether or not you've been to all the great revival meetings, or have known or been related to the great men and women of God or that you've graduated from the best school with honors. What matters is your position before God and how you are with the people He sends your way. This determines your greatness. In whose eyes are you seeking to be great? God's eyes or men's eyes? If you seek God's approval, He'll take care of how people see you. You won't have to worry about it.

Jesus told a parable in Luke 14:7-11 of a wedding feast. He said that when a person is invited to a wedding feast, not to sit in the front seating area but go to the back area. This is so that the person in charge of the wedding does not ask you to go to the back so someone more honorable than you can sit where you sat and you become embarrassed or shamed by the situation. Then if you are to be honored, he will call you to the front and others will also take note of His honor of you. He concludes this parable by saying, **"For whosoever exalteth himself shall be abased; and he that humbleth himself shall be exalted"** (Luke 14:11).

I've seen this happen to people who've presumptuously gone to the front of a setting and then be asked to step back. I've felt for their embarrassment but thought that it could have been avoided had they taken an attitude of humility—being willing and happy to be in the back or the front.

In John 3:30, John the Baptist said, **"He must increase, but I must decrease."** John realized that if God's Kingdom was to come and His will be done, he must be selfless and filled with God.

The big "I" must die! The big "I" has to do with pride. Proverbs 16:18 says, **"Pride goeth before destruction. . . ."** A successful minister must be wary of this subtle tactic of the devil. *God wants you to be successful, but He doesn't want success to have you!*

Thirdly, Jesus humbled Himself. Realize that God won't humble you. You must humble yourself (1 Peter 5:6). There may be times where circumstances become humbling when you go your own way rather than God's way. Even then, however, you must humble yourself in order to receive God's grace, favor and help. God cannot draw unto you if you do not humble yourself. Instead, you will find He will resist you. Where there is a lack of humility to God and to others, life will be very hard (James 4:6).

Fourthly, Jesus was *obedient* to God, His Father, even to the point of laying down His life and dying for the sins of all mankind. Many Christians want to obey as long as it looks good or sounds important. Most Christians do not like uncomfortable or difficult situations. They do everything possible to avoid suffering. Sometimes they've not obeyed God because of the momentary hardship they would face. The problem is when you disobey, ultimately you will end up in prolonged hardship and suffering for your disobedience. Obedience is not always easy at the moment, but disobedience is harder in the long run.

Philippians 2:5 says, **"Let this mind be in you, which was also in Christ Jesus."** We are to have the mind of Christ in the way we think and act. Let's go over it again: 1) He didn't seek a title or reputation; 2) He took upon Himself a servant attitude; 3) He humbled Himself; and 4) He was obedient to God.

"Come, and Learn of Me"

Jesus said, **"Come unto me, all ye that labour and are heavy laden, and I will give you rest. Take my yoke upon you, and *learn of me; for I am meek and lowly in heart*; and ye shall find rest unto your souls"** (Matthew 11:28,29). When we spend time with Jesus daily, we learn how to walk out the life He has called us to live. We get into His yoke instead of trying to do things our way, which causes the yoke to become hard and heavy. Instead, in the midst of difficult situations, we can actually have peace and rest for our souls (our mind, will and emotions).

The illustration of a yoke of oxen is what Jesus is referring to here in this scripture. If you are taking time with Jesus daily, then you are hooking up to His yoke. The lead ox directs which way the second ox goes in pulling a cart. Taking time with Jesus in prayer and in the Word daily helps you to follow His leading through the day. Otherwise, you may find yourself pulling against His leading. When one ox pulls against the other, it will rub the ox to irritation and stop the progress of the cart moving ahead. It is easier to allow the lead ox to lead and the other ox to follow. Progress can happen in this way.

Three Great Men Who Lost Their Leadership Position Because of Pride

Let's look at three kings who didn't seek to walk in a meek spirit: King Saul (1 Samuel, chapters 9-28); King Nebuchadnezzar (Daniel 4); and King Herod (Acts 12:20-23).

1. King Saul was a child of God (Jewish by birth), chosen by God as king, anointed by the prophet Samuel, even used to prophesy at times, but *he wanted to do things his way*, not as God had commanded. First, God lifted the anointing from him, then God could not speak to him anymore because of his pride, and finally both he and his son died so his seed could not reign. The latter years of his life were lived in fear and anger. How sad!

2. King Nebuchadnezzar's *pride* and desire to be above everyone, even God, ended when he went crazy and was changed in his physical appearance. He was sent away from his royal palace to wander like an animal for a period of time *until he humbled himself to God* and began to praise Him as the King of all. His

soundness of mind returned and he was restored to his kingdom.

3. King Herod *felt he had power over everyone* and everything. He had Christians killed. *He loved the applause and fear of men.* One day he went too far in his pride. As he spoke to the crowd of people, they began to say, **"It is the voice of a god, and not of a man"** (Acts 12:22). He accepted it and because he didn't give the glory to God, he was eaten up by worms and died. What a horrible death!

"When pride cometh, then cometh shame: but with the lowly [or humble] **is wisdom"** (Proverbs 11:2). Remember, pride produces shame and humility produces wisdom.

God's Commandments Regarding Meekness

God gives His children many commandments (not options) in His Word concerning meekness:

1. James 1:21 says, **"Receive with meekness the engrafted word, which is able to save your souls."** God taught me a lesson on meekness while my husband and I were attending a summer session of a Bible school. We had been in Tulsa prior to attending this school and had attended another Bible school where we had heard many great teachers of God's Word. Another couple who sat close to us had come to the summer session from California. The speaker for the week was a man we had heard before, and his teaching was on a subject we were already familiar with. While the other couple was elated over the teaching, I was sitting there with a "know-it-all" attitude, thinking to myself, *It's wonderful for all these people to hear this, but I've heard it before and could teach it myself!*

By the second class session, God rebuked me in my heart. He spoke to me that if I kept a meek attitude, even though I had heard these teachings before, I would receive new and vital revelation from these teachers. Immediately I made a quality decision *to keep an open heart to receive God's Word.* No matter how many times you've heard a scripture taught, you can learn more because

God's Word is alive and it will produce more revelation if you allow it to.

Moffatt's Translation of James 1:21 says, **"Make a soil** [in your hearts] **of humble modesty for the Word."** Be good soil! Break up the hard ground!

2. First Peter 3:15 says, **"...be ready always to give an answer to every man that asketh you a reason of the hope that is in you with meekness and fear."** If someone questions you concerning your life as a Christian (and people will when the life of Christ Jesus is reflected through you), respond to them in meekness as you share with them. There are people in the world who have been "turned off" because some Christians have become angry in defending their faith in Jesus Christ.

There have been times when I have witnessed to people who wanted to talk about their discontent with ministers. I've had many opportunities to share information to help them understand and see God's servants differently. At other times when they don't want to understand, I've had to pray for God's wisdom. The goal is to get their focus back on Jesus, not on people.

Sometimes I've encountered people who are more strongly committed to a denomination or a doctrine of belief than to their relationship with Jesus. Usually they want to argue. This is where the servant of the Lord must decide not to enter into the discussion but simply smile and wait for them to pause. Then direct the conversation toward the love and peace of Jesus. Allow some time for them to think about it. Your peaceful and humble spirit will go further than an angry, defensive spirit. They will not forget the attitude of Jesus.

3. Galatians 6:1 says, **"Brethren, if a man be overtaken in a fault, ye which are spiritual, restore such an one in the spirit of meekness; considering thyself, lest thou also be tempted."** In this scripture, Paul was speaking to mature Christians on how to restore another Christian brother or sister who has fallen.

We must bear in mind that we are all human and capable of being tempted. If we keep an attitude of dependency on God's grace, we will be more merciful and seek to help others get back in a strong position with God. If we are condemning toward them or we separate ourselves from them as if to say, "Don't get us dirty with your problem," then we become vulnerable to the devil's attacks. God made us to be a body of believers. When one part suffers, the others are to go to its aid and help restore it. We must take responsibility to help each other.

Second Timothy 2:25,26 NIV says:

Those who oppose him he must gently instruct, in the hope that God will grant them repentance leading them to a knowledge of the truth, and that they will come to their senses and escape from the trap of the devil, who has taken them captive to do his will.

When you and I minister to those who are going through difficult times, we must go with the meekness, humility, and love of our Father God, realizing that we will reap whatever we sow. If we sow mercy, we will reap mercy. Thank God that He is gentle.

4. James 3:13 says, **"Who is a wise man and endued with knowledge among you? let him shew out of a good conversation his works with meekness of wisdom."** *Dake's Reference Bible* says that true wisdom is always accompanied with meekness and gentleness. Proud, overbearing, and disdainful men may pass as scholars and have learning but not true wisdom.[72]

God's Promises to the Meek

"The meek will he guide in judgment: and the meek will he teach his way" (Psalm 25:9). God will guide and teach the meek. He will guide you with His eye. If you're waiting to be led by God, then humble yourself daily before Him and His Word. Become dependent on Him, not on your own talents and education. Obey His Word and the promptings of His Spirit in the small things. Then you'll be quicker to obey Him in big decisions. You will also learn His way of doing things.

Matthew 5:5 says, **"Blessed are the meek: for they shall inherit the earth."** It is the meek person of God who will prosper in every area of life. We've stood on this scripture when believing for property for the ministry. It means you have to keep yourself in a position of meekness so you can believe for it.

"The meek shall eat and be satisfied: they shall praise the Lord that seek him: your heart shall live for ever" (Psalm 22:26). God gives contentment to the person who allows the fruit of meekness to rule him. He wants His children to be satisfied and to be praising and grateful sons and daughters.

Endotes

[70] Dake, p. 206.

[71] Vine, pp. 727, 728.

[72] Dake, p. 262.

CHAPTER 13
SELF-CONTROL

But the fruit of the [Holy] Spirit [the work which His presence within accomplishes] is ... *self-control* **(self-restraint, continence)....**

Galatians 5:22,23 AMP

Self-control or *temperance* in the Greek is *enkrateia* and means moderation in the indulgence of the appetites and passions.[73] Webster defines *temperance* as moderate in indulging the appetites; not self-indulgent; moderate in one's actions, speech, etc.; self-restrained; characterized by moderation or restraint.[74]

Earlier in chapter 1, we discussed how that we, as humans, are a three-part being. If you build up your spirit, then your spirit will be able to control your soul (reasoning, thoughts, emotions and will) and your body. If you do not build up your spirit, then your soul and body will dominate your life. Your soul and body will then convince you to do what feels good at the moment or what looks easiest and most convenient. The soul and body will also convince you that no one will ever know, or what difference will it make to do a little of whatever you want to do.

Some Christians never learn to walk in self-control because they don't take time to build up their spirit man. They learn to shove aside the still, small voice of the Holy Spirit speaking to them and instead follow their emotions or their own desires and reasoning. Sometimes they may even put a religious coat on it and say that they felt God led them to do what they did, when in fact, if they closely examined what they did, they would know that it goes against the principles of God's Word.

In order to walk in the Spirit and be like Jesus, we will have to exercise self-control. We will have to learn to say "no" to that which pulls on our flesh and emotions to sin.

We are definitely in a battle spiritually against the devil. First Peter 2:11 AMP says, **"Beloved, I implore you as aliens and strangers and exiles [in this world] to abstain from the sensual urges (the evil desires, the passions of the flesh, your lower nature) that wage war against the soul."**

Jesus experienced this battle and overcame so that we could see how to overcome the devil. Through the power of God's Spirit and the Word of God, Jesus walked in the fruit of self-control.

If we are Jesus people, then we are called to exercise the same self-restraint or self-control that He exercised. The scripture tells us in Hebrews 4:15 that Jesus **"...was in all points tempted like as we are, yet without sin."** In Matthew 4:1-11 and Luke 4:1-13, it is recorded that Jesus was led up by the Spirit into the wilderness to fast and pray. There He was tempted of the devil. Realizing His need for food and His physical weakness, Satan came with the three temptations that he had tempted Adam and Eve with in the garden: the lust of the flesh, the lust of the eyes and the pride of life.

We must realize the enemy watches to come with temptation at strategic times. Notice, he came to Jesus right after Jesus had been fasting. It was a spiritually intense time communing with His Father God, and Jesus was physically weak and hungry. This meant that the temptations were greater to resist because of physical weakness.

During a time of fasting and praying, people open their spirits up to hear from God, so right after such a time, people are still open to hear other voices speaking, too. We must guard ourselves from hearing the stranger's voice deceptively telling us to do something that is not God's direction. We must ask ourselves, "Does this feed the flesh or pride? Is it something that could hurt others or help them?" Anything that the Spirit of God says will be for good purposes. It will reflect a servant heart attitude and will be from pure motives. It will not be "self-centered" but "others-centered."

Jesus overcame each temptation with the spoken Word. Each time He said, "It is written." By speaking the Word, Jesus resisted Satan, overcame him and the devil left Him for a season.

In this account, Jesus gave us the key to resisting temptation and overcoming Satan. He could have used supernatural power to get rid of him, but instead, He gave us the spiritual keys for overcoming the devil so any believer could do it, too.

The first key is *prayer*. Jesus had a relationship with God through prayer. Prayer is simply talking to God and listening to Him. In Matthew 26:36-41, Jesus had taken His disciples to the garden of Gethsemane to pray. After praying awhile, He walked over to where the disciples were asleep and said to Peter, **"What, could ye not watch with me one hour? Watch and pray, that ye enter not into temptation: the spirit indeed is willing, but the flesh is weak"** (vv. 40,41).

Prayer and watchfulness (or spiritual sensitivity) are vital in order to resist temptation. We're living in a world of temptation that constantly makes it easy for the flesh to do whatever it wants to do. Christians who do not take an active stand of resistance will be overcome.

In our early years of pastoring, I had become friends with a lady in the church who had children the same age as my children. When we visited she shared her testimony of how God had delivered her from alcohol, drugs and sexual immorality. She also had a real burden for unwed mothers and a desire to have a ministry to these young women because she had been one at one time.

She and her family ended up leaving the church because of the convenience of going somewhere else. Gradually they dropped out of church altogether. Later, she and her husband divorced. She began dating again and got involved in alcohol and sexual immorality. The day came when she had too much to drink and was in a fatal accident.

When they began to go to church out of convenience, they became less active toward a daily time in the Word and in prayer. Apparently they did not realize that being in God's will regarding church attendance, prayer and God's Word are key elements for resisting the devil. If we are going to overcome the devil to the end as the book of Revelation exhorts us, we must stay in a position of active resistance. Apathy and passivity are open doors to the devil's deception.

The second key to resisting the devil is *speaking the Word of God.* In 1974 my husband and I heard a message on confessing God's Word that changed our lives and became a foundational truth we have kept and acted upon through the years in every area of our lives. I believe it has delivered us over and over again.

If you've never learned to pray God's Word, start now. Find scriptures to speak over your life and speak them with faith each day over you and your loved ones, your work, your ministry and over others. The spoken Word is the most powerful weapon against the devil. Hebrews 4:12 says it is like a two-edged sword.

At that time, the two-edged sword was the most powerful weapon known to man. Since then other more powerful weapons have been created. If it were written today, it would be compared to the computerized missile. An enemy cannot escape this powerful weapon's ability to seek and destroy. In the same way, God's Word destroys Satan's plots and schemes when we believe and speak it in prayer.

Revelation 12:11 tells us that we overcome the devil by the blood of the Lamb and the word of our testimony. *We can keep our lives in self-control as we believe and speak God's Word.* We can overcome the works of the flesh as we choose to follow Jesus. First Peter 4:1,2 AMP says:

So, since Christ suffered in the flesh for us, for you, arm yourselves with the same thought and purpose [patiently to suffer rather than fail to please God]. For whoever has suffered in the flesh [having the mind of Christ] is done with [intentional] sin [has stopped

pleasing himself and the world, and pleases God],

So that he can no longer spend the rest of his natural life living by [his] human appetites and desires, but [he lives] for what God wills.

Paul's Comparison of Self-Control with Olympic Athletes

Paul recognized that every Christian must exercise self-restraint and inward strength if he is to run the race of life successfully.

Do you not know that in a race all the runners compete, but [only] one receives the prize? So run [your race] that you may lay hold [of the prize] and make it yours.

Now every athlete who goes into training conducts himself temperately and restricts himself in all things. They do it to win a wreath that will soon wither, but we [do it to receive a crown of eternal blessedness] that cannot wither.

Therefore I do not run uncertainly (without definite aim). I do not box like one beating the air and striking without an adversary.

But [like a boxer] I buffet my body [handle it roughly, discipline it by hardships] and subdue it, for fear that after proclaiming to others the Gospel and things pertaining to it, I myself should become unfit [not stand the test, be unapproved and rejected as a counterfeit].

1 Corinthians 9:24-27 AMP

Paul was making a comparison between the Olympic games of his day and the spiritual race of the Christian. In an Olympic game, only one could receive the prize. In the race God has set before us, we are all eligible to win! We are not competing against *each other*, but we are running (competing) against time and against the weights and traps of sin and the devil.

Paul wants us to envision an actual race so we will press toward the mark for the prize of the high calling of God in Christ Jesus (Philippians 3:14). What Paul is saying is that we, as Christians, must have the same compelling determination for highest excellence as the Olympic athlete has for his endeavors. It is not enough just to wear the name "Christian." Paul exhorts us to make the effort to live the Christian life. He exhorts us to see ourselves as athletes in training. An athlete in training *keeps himself or herself in a self-restricted lifestyle* compared to other people. While non-athletes eat and drink whatever they desire, stay up late to party, do not exercise and make no effort to improve their physical well-being, the athlete thinks about and avoids eating and drinking anything that could slow him down. He gets proper rest even if he has to miss a party. He exercises daily, realizing muscles cannot lie dormant or they lose strength, firmness and flexibility.

As Christians we are to take responsibility to avoid situations that could pull us down spiritually. We must guard ourselves spiritually to not let our "output" of works squeeze out our "input" time with the Lord daily. This input time is our rest and refreshing to be strong for all we encounter.

(Note: There is a balance to be kept of receiving personally from time alone with the Lord and receiving from conferences, campmeetings and seminars. Some people try to go to every "spiritual party" or gathering and never have enough time alone with Jesus to have character built in their lives. Others may think that they can only get revelation straight from God to themselves and do not value the ministry gifts of others in the Body of Christ whom God wants to use to speak into their lives. Learn to follow the leading of the Holy Spirit rather than being driven by preconceived thoughts or by your emotions.)

Paul said, "I don't run uncertainly or without a definite aim." Our aim or goal in life is to "be like Jesus." Your "being" is more important than your "doing." Why? Because your "being" will affect your "doing," and you'll "do" the things God wants instead of "doing out of the effort of the flesh."

Paul went on to say that he disciplined his body by hardships in order to subdue it (1 Corinthians 9:27 AMP). Many Christians feel they deserve that everything be comfortable. If you stay in the comfort zone, you won't grow. Get out beyond your comfort zone where you have to use your faith and work some spiritual muscles that you've never worked. Get out where you have to do things you've never done before. Let your "hands get a little dirty or tougher" by helping in situations that no one else wants to handle. Stretch yourself so God can do more in and through your life.

Paul said that he didn't want to preach the Gospel and become so at ease that he became unfit, disqualified and rejected as a counterfeit (1 Corinthians 9:27 AMP). Paul was also aware that just because he had been saved did not mean that he could live life casually. He knew that if he allowed his body and emotions to rule his life, he could become a *castaway*. The word *castaway* in the Greek is *adokimos*, which means reprobate, Christless and literally rejected.[75]

We read that every man who *strives* for the mastery is temperate (self-controlled) in *all* things. The word *strive* connotes to make great effort, to be in conflict, struggle, contend, fight, compete.[76] The word *mastery* has the meaning of mastership, rule, control, victory in struggle or competition; to get the upper hand; to become expert in skill or knowledge.[77] God wants your spirit man to master your soul and body.

Paul is saying that we as Christians are to make great effort to contend for the Word of God in our lives. In this we gain victories over and over again and become more and more skillful and knowledgeable of God's Word, applying it to our lives and to the situations we face. Thus, the Kingdom of God increases in and through us as the Body of Christ.

Second Peter 1:5,6 AMP says:

For this very reason, adding your diligence [to the divine promises], employ every effort in exercising your faith to develop virtue (excellence, resolution,

Christian energy), and in [exercising] virtue [develop] knowledge (intelligence),

And in [exercising] knowledge [develop] self-control....

You Take Control By Your Choice

As Christians, we are to take control of what we see, hear and read, and whom we allow to influence our lives. We are responsible for our emotions, impulses and desires. For example, circumstances may press your emotions to respond negatively, but through the fruit of self-control, you *choose* to respond differently. You *choose* to walk in peace while others may want to argue. You *choose* to forgive and show mercy when others offend, disappoint, or fail you. You *choose* to keep the joy of the Lord when you feel unhappy. You *choose* not to speak when your emotions are wanting your mouth to speak. All of these are examples of self-control in operation.

Some may say, "Well, I believe you should vent your emotions." There have been so many people today who have vented their emotions that we have destruction everywhere— destroyed marriages, destroyed family relationships, murders, broken hearts, depressed and abused personalities, etc. Some people have vented their emotions and later regretted ever saying or doing what they said and did but cannot change it now.

Get control by submitting to God's Word in your life personally. There are those who have learned that freedom is not doing whatever you feel at the moment. Freedom is in choosing to walk in love toward God and others. Galatians 5:13 AMP says, **"For you, brethren, were [indeed] called to freedom; only [do not let your] freedom be an incentive to your flesh and an opportunity *or excuse [for selfishness]*, but through love you should serve one another."** *The love walk requires self-control!*

Jesus said in Luke 17:1 that offenses would come. He also said in John 16:33, **"In the world ye shall have tribulation: but**

be of good cheer [rejoice in the midst of it]; **I have overcome the world."** He said that He spoke these things to us so we would have peace. *Walking in peace demands self-control!* All of the fruit of the Spirit require self-control.

A fellow once said, "I have no trouble walking with God in the Christian life. It's just all the other Christians I have problems with!" That sounds funny, but that's really the way some people feel. In becoming a part of the family of God, we must learn to live together as family. God can use other brothers and sisters in the Lord to develop fruit in our lives if we allow Him to. We may not always appreciate the part they are playing in our spiritual growth, but we will realize it is a way God works the rough edges off of us. I've experienced this in my life, and I know of others who have grown in the fruit of the Spirit because they've had to learn patience and understanding with me.

Hebrews 10:24,25 says:

> **And let us *consider* one another to *provoke* unto love and to good works:**
>
> **Not forsaking the assembling of ourselves together, as the manner of some is; but exhorting one another: and so much the more, as ye see the day approaching.**

The word *consider*, as used in verse 24, means to discover and behold one another in order to *provoke* (in the Greek it means to urge, prick, irritate, excite and make keener) one another to love and to do good works. You may feel that some Christians provoke you too much, but if you'll go to Jesus, He'll show you how they are actually helping you grow in Him and in your love walk.

The Lord then tells us not to forsake assembling together with the Body of Christ. You need others in the Body of Christ in spite of your feelings and emotions. Jesus made us a body with many parts. You cannot say, "I don't need or want that part." (See 1 Corinthians 12:14-27.) The way to grow in the fruit of the Spirit is to be around other people. You aren't forced to grow or change as long as you remain a loner, or are consistently with people who always agree with you and never challenge you in any way.

What's Inside of You Will Come Out

Put the Word of God in you daily by reading it, praying it and meditating it so that when you're being tested in the fruit of the Spirit, it will come out of your mouth. The illustration of a lemon and an orange can help us understand this principle. Both are pretty on the outside. However, if you cut and squeeze them, what comes out of them is different. Sour juice comes out of a lemon, but sweet juice comes out of an orange. Did the cut and the squeeze cause the lemon to be sour? No. Cutting and squeezing the lemon just revealed what was inside of it. The cutting and squeezing come when others challenge you, offend you, or irritate you.

What is inside of you? Have you put the Word of God in you so that when you are cut and squeezed, His nature flows out of you? Or have you been saved and had some wonderful Christian experiences but haven't been putting the Word of God in your life, thinking that you look pretty good? Like the lemon, you may look as good as the orange, but believe me, you will get cut and squeezed and everyone will then find out what's inside of you.

The Tongue

One of the major areas of a person's life to get control of is the tongue. This is one area that I am constantly having to guard and keep corrected. The reason is that the Bible says it controls the whole body. James says that the tongue is like a bit in a horse's mouth or like the small helm of a ship. The bit controls the movement of the horse; the helm controls the course of the ship. (See James 3:1-10.) Your words can create or destroy the atmosphere of love, joy and peace. Your words can bring peace, comfort, strength and encouragement, or they can bring strife, anger, hurt, pain, discouragement and weakness.

The tongue, although a very small member of the body, controls, directs and sets the course for the body. If the tongue is left without control, it is a world of iniquity and is set on fire of hell (James 3:6). Like a fire, it can destroy. Without putting God's Word in his heart daily, man has a tendency to use his tongue for gossip, strife, criticism and backbiting. Christians have been guilty of using their tongue as a destructive force, because they have lacked control of their tongue.

Along with putting God's Word into your heart daily, you must act upon the Word. You must choose to do what the Word says. It says, **"...the servant of the Lord must not strive..."** (2 Timothy 2:24). It says, **"Do not let any unwholesome talk come out of your mouths, but only what is helpful for building others up according to their needs, that it may benefit those who listen"** (Ephesians 4:29 NIV). The Word says, **"Let all bitterness and indignation and wrath (passion, rage, bad temper) and resentment (anger, animosity) and quarreling (brawling, clamor, contention) and slander (evil speaking, abusive or blasphemous language) be banished from you, with all malice (spite, ill will, or baseness of any kind)"** (Ephesians 4:31 AMP).

In order to obey these words from God, we must exercise self-control and self-restraint. Taking time to pray will also subdue our emotions and help us respond with control as we speak to others.

Anger Can Be Conquered

"He that is slow to anger is better than the mighty; and he that ruleth his spirit than he that taketh a city" (Proverbs 16:32). When you are being tempted to get into anger, take a moment to stop and pray quietly in the Spirit to keep your emotions under control. You will calm down and sense your spirit man taking control over your feelings. Even if you still are disturbed within, you'll sense God's help to control yourself. Before discussing a definite disagreement with someone else, if you can sleep on it one night, then speak to the person the next day, this will stop a lot of emotional uprisings. If this is not possible, make a conscious effort to speak with peace and excuse yourself before getting emotional so that you can go somewhere to pray and let God calm you.

"Be ye angry, and sin not: let not the sun go down upon your wrath" (Ephesians 4:26). Righteous anger is a godly emotion expressed against sin. (Jesus showed divine anger toward the moneychangers in the Temple.) However, it is extremely important that you do not confuse human anger with godly anger. Some people have tried to cover up their personal anger, excusing it as righteous indignation when, in actuality, it is the wrath of man. James 1:19,20 AMP puts it this way:

Understand [this], my beloved brethren. Let every man be quick to hear [a ready listener], slow to speak, slow to take offense and to get angry.

For man's anger does not promote the righteousness God [wishes and requires].

While people in the world around us are trying to conquer "outer space," it would be good to focus some effort on conquering "inner space." In a society of abuse, God desires that Christians lift up a standard of righteousness against the flood of the enemy's attack on people. Part of that standard is that we have self-control over our emotions and show others that there is a better way to live. God's will for homes is peace, not abuse of one another. Abuse, whether it is verbal, physical, or sexual, should not be named among Christians. It is not normal and it is not Christian. Jesus Christ never abused anyone. He corrected, rebuked and instructed people out of love, but He did not abuse them.

Stopping Jealousy

Years ago, a couple came to our church and attended a marriage seminar which we held. The wife confided in me that her husband had a problem with jealousy of her. She could not even say hello to a man without him feeling jealous. I talked to them about coming for further marriage counseling, and they agreed to come. After one session, he didn't feel the need to return.

The company for which he worked then moved them to another state. The wife stayed in touch with one of our staff ladies. Within one year after they moved, he killed her and ended up in prison. Why? Because he never brought his emotions into submission to God and never allowed himself to become accountable to others for his life. We cannot allow our emotions and thoughts to go unrestrained.

We are called to be Jesus people. You have Him living inside of you. His Spirit within is enough to live victorious over the spirit of this world system. Give Jesus a place, but give the devil no place! **"Ye are of God, little children, and have overcome them: because greater is he that is in you, than he that is in the world"** (1 John 4:4).

Moderation vs. Excess

Another aspect of the fruit of self-control or temperance is to live your life in moderation. Some things are not sinful, but if we do them in excess and allow them to take priority, sometimes these things gradually steal our time with God. There is a need for us to be moderate in many areas of life.

Philippians 4:5 says, **"Let your moderation be known unto all men. The Lord is at hand."** Notice, Paul says people should know your moderation. Can people see your moderation in the way you conduct yourself? We should not only realize that the Lord is coming soon, but He is here with us right now. He is observing us, as are other people. Living in moderation is having a consciousness of His presence and what He would want you to do. Are you seeking to please Him, or are you just living your life the way you want to live it?

For example, food is a necessity in life, but some people eat

151

as much as they want and beyond and become what the Bible calls "a glutton." Proverbs 23:2 says, **"And put a knife to thy throat, if thou be a man given to appetite."** Verse 21 says, **"For the drunkard and the glutton shall come to poverty. . . ."**

First Corinthians 6:12,13 says:

All things are lawful unto me, but all things are not expedient: all things are lawful for me, but I will not be brought under the power of any.

Meats for the belly, and the belly for meats: but God shall destroy both it and them....

As a Christian, since it is Jesus we are seeking to please, our moderation will affect how we eat, drink and dress; how much time we spend doing things, whether or not something is beneficial or just a time robber; where we go; how much we work or spend on leisure and entertainment, etc. Moderation helps us not to get entangled with the distractions of this life. Keeping our lives in balance and exercising self-restraint will help us make wiser decisions and be more discerning.

No man that warreth entangleth himself with the affairs of this life; that he may please him who hath chosen him to be a soldier.

2 Timothy 2:4

Not only is self-control for our benefit personally, but it benefits other people who are watching our lives. Every believer has people around them who are watching how they respond and react in daily life. Although most Christians don't want to feel responsible for others, Scripture indicates that we are. This is not a bondage, because freedom is walking in the love of God toward others. It is taking our responsibility as Christians.

Romans 14:13-15 AMP says:

...endeavor never to put a stumbling block or an obstacle or a hindrance in the way of a brother.

I know and am convinced (persuaded) as one in the Lord Jesus, that nothing is [forbidden as] essentially unclean (defiled and unholy in itself). But [none the

less] it is unclean (defiled and unholy) to anyone who thinks it is unclean.

But if your brother is being pained or his feelings hurt or if he is being injured by what you eat, [then] you are no longer walking in love. [You have ceased to be living and conducting yourself by the standard of love toward him.] Do not let what you eat hurt or cause the ruin of one for whom Christ died!

A person who lives in moderation is emotionally stronger in coping with life and usually is content, while a person who does not learn moderation usually is discontented. People who do not exercise self-restraint and who do whatever they want are not easy to work with or to live with. This is because usually they are not considerate of others, but their focus is on themselves. Moderation is necessary if we are going to walk in the love of God.

Who's Controlling Your Mind?

The fruit of the Spirit, *self-control*, begins by renewing your mind to think according to the Word of God. Then, like Proverbs 23:7 says, **"For as he thinketh in his heart, so is he. . . ."** You will become what you think.

Romans 12:2 says:

And be not conformed to this world: but be ye transformed by the renewing of your mind, that ye may prove what is that good, and acceptable, and perfect, will of God.

Your mind is the battlefield of your life. You can capture your thoughts and make them think on whatever you choose, so make them think according to the Word of God.

Second Corinthians 10:3-5 says:

For though we walk in the flesh, we do not war after the flesh:

(For the weapons of our warfare are not carnal, but mighty through God to the pulling down of strong holds;)

Casting down imaginations, and every high thing that exalteth itself against the knowledge of God, and bringing into captivity every thought to the obedience of Christ.

If it means putting a TV in a closet for a season or even, for some, getting rid of it in order to guard one's thoughts and desires, then do it. If it means not having the Internet on your computer, then don't have it. If it means not shopping at certain stores where you are tempted to buy their magazines, then don't go there. First Thessalonians 5:22 says, **"Abstain** [remove yourself or get away] **from all appearance of evil."** If it means cutting off relationships that pull you down, then cut them off. Guard your thoughts, emotions and desires.

I've known Christians who thought that as long as they kept what they viewed in secret, no one would ever find out. The problem is, they viewed it long enough until they acted it out and others were hurt. Get control of your thoughts before it's too late.

Paul wrote to the church at Rome in Romans 1:18-32 that there were those who became so vain in their imaginations and their foolish hearts were darkened that God gave them over to a reprobate mind and let them go ahead and do what they knew was wrong. They refused to understand and became heartless and unforgiving. They were fully aware of God's death penalty for those who did the things they did, but they went right ahead and did them anyway and encouraged others to sin along with them.[78]

The devil throws wrong thoughts at *every* Christian daily. One minister said, "Just because birds fly over your head does not mean you have to let them stop and build a nest in your hair." Cast down those thoughts by telling them, "No, that can have no place in my mind," and tell yourself that you are going to think on whatever is true, honest, just, pure, lovely, of good report, virtuous and praiseworthy. (See Philippians 4:8.)

Just because a wrong thought comes does not mean you have sinned. If you cast it down immediately, you have used your fruit of self-control and you've not sinned. However, if you allow the wrong thought to linger (build a nest) in your mind and you meditate upon it, then you've sinned and you need to repent to God and receive His cleansing blood to remove it. Then choose to think differently *according to the Word of God.* It is in your power to choose to think on good things that are edifying.

Remember, God will always be there to encourage you so you can overcome and gain control. Never quit because you fail. Just get back on the Word immediately.

Mortify the Deeds of the Flesh

Colossians 3:5-10 NKJV says, "**Therefore put to death your members which are on the earth: fornication, uncleanness, passion, evil desire, and covetousness, which is idolatry. Because of these things the wrath of God is coming upon the sons of disobedience, in which you yourselves once walked when you lived in them. But now you yourselves are to put off all these: anger, wrath, malice, blasphemy, filthy language out of your mouth. Do not lie to one another, since you have put off the old man with his deeds, and have put on the new *man* who is renewed in knowledge according to the image of Him who created him.**"

How does a person mortify the deeds of their flesh? *Mortify* means to deaden, subdue, conquer, vanquish, defeat and force to submit. Paul said in Romans 6:11, after you receive Jesus Christ as Lord and Savior, "**reckon yourselves to be <u>dead to sin</u> but alive unto God through our Lord and Savior Jesus Christ.**"

Believe you've been set free, cleansed by the blood of Jesus, and that you are a new creation in Christ. Then don't allow any opportunity for the temptation of your flesh to do whatever it did before (Rom. 13:14). Begin to renew your mind with scripture by reading, memorizing, and speaking it in prayer over your life daily. Listen to scripture on CDs. The scripture cleanses our minds and creates a new way of thinking in us. Avoid any situations that would pull on the lust of your flesh. In other words, don't go near whatever tempts you. Fasting with prayer at times of testing can strengthen you. The Psalmist wrote, **"I humbled my soul with fasting"** (Psalm 35:13). God gives graces to the humble (James 4:6). Grace is the divine empowerment from God to do His will. His grace will be there for you to help you resist temptation and help you stop and think about the consequences so that you will choose to do the right thing.

Learn to obey the promptings of the voice of the Holy Spirit immediately and not shove them aside. The more you obey these thoughts, the stronger you'll become. Remember, self-control is not only about our present life but also our eternity. Keep mindful of eternity. Second Corinthians 5:10 TLB says, **"For we must all stand before Christ to be judged and have our lives laid bare before Him. Each of us will receive whatever he deserves for the good or bad things he has done in his earthly body."**

One man said, "True self-control means a willingness to resign the small for the sake of the great, the present for the sake of the future, the material for the sake of the spiritual and that is what faith makes possible" – Hugh Black.

"And the world passes away and disappears, and with it the forbidden cravings (the passionate desires, the lust) of it; but he who does the will of God and carries out His purposes in his life abides (remains) forever" (1 John 2:17 AMP).

Helpful Guidelines for Self-Control

Here are a few guidelines for helping you to strengthen the fruit of *self-control* in your life:

1.   Self-control starts with receiving Jesus Christ as Lord and Savior. When you live in a kingdom under the rulership

of a king, he now owns you and has the right or authority to rule you. You cannot just do whatever you want to do. Instead, you ask him what you can or cannot do.

2. Self-control requires <u>submission</u> to God's authority. James 4:7 says, **"Therefore submit to God. Resist the devil and he will flee from you."**

3. Self-control grows by building up your spirit man through self-discipline. (1 Cor. 9:24-27).

   a. Take time daily in the Word. **"Wherewithal shall a young man cleanse his way? by taking heed thereto according to thy word. . .Thy word have I hid in mine heart, that I might not sin against thee"** (Psalm 119:9,11).

   b. Take time daily in prayer. **"Watch and pray, that ye enter not into temptation: the spirit indeed is willing, but the flesh is weak"** (Matthew 26:41). In your daily prayer time, pray scripture over your life. Also, pray in the spirit – **"But you, beloved, building yourselves up on your most holy faith, praying in the Holy Spirit"** (Jude 20 NKJV). First Corinthians 14:15 says, **"...I will pray with the spirit, and I will also pray with the understanding. I will sing with the spirit, and I will also sing with the understanding."** When you renew your mind to the Word of God and pray, it enables you to discern and to control your soul (mind, reasoning, thoughts, will, emotions, passions and desires). Otherwise, you will be out of control. Being out of control may seem easier at the moment, but it will bring the fruit of heartache and pain later on.

4. <u>Mortify</u> = to subdue, conquer and force the flesh to submit to the urgings and the power of the Holy Spirit who is now with you. **"Mortify therefore your members which are upon the earth; fornication, uncleanness, inordinate affection, evil concupiscence, and covetousness, which**

is idolatry" (Col. 3:5).

5. Be sensitive in your spirit to hear God. **"...To day if ye will hear his voice, harden not your hearts..."** (Hebrews 3:7,8).

6. Be righteous-conscious. Remember, having an attitude of righteousness in Jesus makes you want to stay right with Him. **"For he hath made him to be sin for us, who knew no sin; that we might be made the righteousness of God in him"** (2 Corinthians 5:21).

7. Be quick to repent if you sin, and reckon yourself dead to sin and alive unto God. **"If we confess our sins, he is faithful and just to forgive us our sins, and to cleanse us from all unrighteousness"** (1 John 1:9). **"Likewise reckon ye also yourselves to be dead indeed unto sin, but alive unto God through Jesus Christ our Lord"** (Romans 6:11). **"I am crucified with Christ: nevertheless I live; yet not I, but Christ liveth in me: and the life which I now live in the flesh I live by the faith of the Son of God, who loved me, and gave himself for me"** (Galatians 2:20).

8. Guard your heart and guard your mind. Don't let wrong thoughts stay in your mind. Get rid of them. Cast down wrong thoughts. **"For though we walk in the flesh, we do not war after the flesh: For the weapons of our warfare are not carnal, but mighty through God to the pulling down of strong holds; casting down imaginations, and every high thing that exalteth itself against the knowledge of God, and bringing into captivity every thought to the obedience of Christ"** (2 Corinthians 10:3-5). Think on thoughts that line up with God's Word. **"Finally, brethren, whatsoever things are true, whatsoever things are honest, whatsoever things are just, whatsoever things are pure, whatsoever things are lovely, whatsoever things are of good report; if there be any virtue, and if there be any praise, think on these things"** (Philippians 4:8). **"Keep and guard your heart**

with all vigilance and above all that you guard, for out of it flow the springs of life" (Proverbs 4:23 AMP).

9. Keep humble before God. "...God resisteth the proud, but giveth grace unto the humble" (James 4:6).

10. Set your affections upon the Lord. "If ye then be risen with Christ, seek those things which are above, where Christ sitteth on the right hand of God" (Colossians 3:1).

Endotes

[73] Ibid., p. 206.

[74] Webster, p. 1464.

[75] Dake, p. 182.

[76] Webster, p. 1412.

[77] Ibid., p. 873.

[78] *Holy Spirit Encounter Bible, New Living Translation,* (Lake Mary, FL: Creation House, 1996), (Romans 1:24-32), p. 1073.

CHAPTER 14
ABIDING IN THE VINE

Abide in me, and I in you. As the branch cannot bear fruit of itself, except it abide in the vine; no more can ye, except ye abide in me"** (John 15:4). *The Amplified Translation* of this verse says, **"*Dwell* in Me, and I will *dwell* in you. [Live in Me, and I will live in you.] Just as no branch can bear fruit of itself without abiding in (being vitally united to) the vine, neither can you bear fruit unless you abide in Me."**

According to *Webster's New World Dictionary*, to *abide* means "to remain; to stand fast; to go on being; to submit to and carry out (a rule, decision, etc.); to live up to (a promise, agreement, etc.); to continue; to stay." Webster says to see also "bide," which means "to stay or continue and has a sense of *compelling oneself to stay or reside or dwell.*"[79]

Jesus said in John 8:31 AMP, **"...If you abide in My word [hold fast to My teachings and live in accordance with them], you are truly My disciples."** There is a definite difference in being just a believer in Jesus and in being a disciple of Jesus. First John 2:6 AMP says, **"Whoever says he abides in Him ought [as a personal debt] to walk and conduct himself in the same way in which He walked and conducted Himself."** You see, a disciple is one who *abides* and *continues* in following the doctrine and lifestyle of his Master and Teacher, Jesus.

Many people who truly have had a born-again experience have failed to go on to become a disciple of the Lord. The same was true in Jesus' day. In the sixth chapter of John, Jesus told the multitudes that He was the Bread of Life. He spoke in spiritual

161

parallels they did not understand, nor did they try to understand. Scripture says, "**From that time many of his disciples went back, and walked no more with him**" (John 6:66).

The twelve disciples remained, even though they did not fully understand what Jesus was saying. They realized, however, that Jesus had the words of life. Although you may not fully understand the Word of God at this time, continue diligently in the Word and you will come to a knowledge of the truth and thereby walk in the freedom that He promised.

In the Greek, the word *abide* is *meno*, meaning that which remains stable and steadfast; that which dwells, remains and continues.[80] If a Christian does not have a daily time with God in the Word and in prayer, he or she will not become stable and steadfast. Instead, they will be "roller coaster" Christians. They'll be up as long as they are in a good church meeting or with stronger Christian friends. But they'll be down emotionally and succumb to temptation and sin the next day when they are not in that emotionally high atmosphere or with their Christian friends.

The Word of God enables us to be stable—not changing our attitudes, actions, or lifestyle—regardless of the circumstances in which we find ourselves. In other words, we are not to be like a chameleon, which is a lizard whose skin color changes according to the environment it is in.

Your personality should not change from the church service to your home or to your workplace. You are to remain the same. The only way to do this is by putting God's Word in your mind and in your heart. God's Word is so alive and powerful, it will transform your personality into the image of your Savior and Lord, Jesus Christ. His Word renews your mind to think differently so that you will act accordingly.

Proverbs 23:7 says, "**For as he thinketh in his heart, so is he.**" In order to act out (or walk out) the fruit of the Spirit, you will have to keep renewing your mind with God's Word.

I was converted to Christ as a teenager. I'd always been in church because my father was a pastor. I loved God, but I didn't read the Bible. I didn't realize that if you really love Him, you will also love His Word (John 14:23,24). After my conversion, I felt impressed in my heart to read the Bible each day. To my amazement, I no longer wondered about my salvation. I knew that I knew that I was saved (1 John 5:11). Later, I found out the reason for my assurance was that I had the *record* and I was spending time studying it daily. Most Christians who fall away from God do so by neglecting the record of God's Word.

Another truth I've come to realize is that no matter how many times I've read through the Bible, I must have it each day if I am going to live a *stable* Christian life. No one has ever arrived at a place where they can go on the years of study they have had and not continue in the Word daily.

God's Word is life to us (Proverbs 4:22). If it is life, then in order to live we must have it. Matthew 4:4 says, **"...Man shall not live by bread alone, but by every word that proceedeth out of the mouth of God."**

Romans 12:2 exhorts us, **"And be not conformed to this world: but be ye transformed by the renewing of your mind** [with the Word of God], **that ye may prove what is that good, and acceptable, and perfect, will of God."**

John 15:4 says that a branch can't bear fruit unless it abides in the vine. An amazing thing that I came to realize about grapevines is that over a period of years, the branches which grow on a grapevine begin to look like the vine itself. Likewise, as you and I (the branches) continue in the Word of God (the Vine), we will begin to look more and more like Jesus!

Jesus and the Word are one. John 1:14 says, ***"And the Word was made flesh, and dwelt among us,* (and we beheld his glory, the glory as of the only begotten of the Father,) full of grace and truth."** This truth has absolutely changed my life. By putting God's Word in my life, His Word can become flesh in me. His life can grow in me and cause me to be His witness in the earth to others.

Seeing Jesus

I had a hard time trying to understand the old song, "Turn your eyes upon Jesus, look full in His wonderful face; and the things of earth will grow strangely dim, in the light of His glory and grace." I wanted to see Jesus, but I didn't know how. When I discovered that I could see Jesus in His Word, then I realized how the things of this earth can grow dim or lose their influence on my life. I also realized that we can envision Him in worship and prayer, but the Word of God is the stability to which we cling.

As we abide or take time daily to put God's Word in our hearts, then throughout the day that Word holds us in accountability. The Word exposes wrong thoughts, attitudes, or directions that we may have in our lives. His Word becomes like reins on a horse. Jesus is able to help us think, do and say the right things if we are abiding in Him.

I remember a deeply moving story that illustrates this truth. A little boy was standing in a subway station holding a boxed jigsaw puzzle. A businessman came running through the subway station trying to catch the last train that would get him to work on time. As he ran past the little boy, he accidentally knocked the box containing the puzzle out of his hands, scattering the pieces all over the subway station floor.

The hurrying executive stopped, quickly scanned the little boy's face, the scattered puzzle pieces, and his train, which was slowly pulling out of the station. He had to make a fast decision—whether to be late for his job or to assist the startled little boy. He put his briefcase down and began to retrieve the puzzle pieces for the boy.

The little boy lifted his eyes from the box as the man dropped in a few pieces and asked, "Mister, are you Jesus?"

Wow! What if he had hurried away? Would that little boy have seen Jesus that day? Second Corinthians 3:2,3 says that we are living epistles of Christ, known and read of all men. The name *Christian* actually means "Christlike." The more we abide in Him, the more like Christ we will become. Others will then be able to see Jesus in us. We'll take time to stop and think how Jesus would want us to react or respond.

You and I, the branches, are extensions of the Vine. The branches by themselves cannot produce fruit. They must be connected to the Vine. And the Vine is the Source of life; the branches simply bear the fruit. Mary, the mother of Jesus, did not produce Jesus. God produced Jesus within her womb. She was the yielded vessel who carried Jesus and then bore Him out to the world. Spiritually speaking, we are vessels of God, carrying Jesus and bearing Him out to the world. As we abide in the Word of God, we will be more sensitive in expressing the nature of Jesus to others.

God's Word Creates a Desire Not to Sin

As you meditate in God's Word, allow it to dwell in you richly, for then sin cannot have a strong hold in your life. Scripture says, *"No one who abides in Him* [who lives and remains in communion with and in obedience to Him—*deliberately, knowingly, and habitually] commits (practices) sin.* No one who [habitually] sins has either seen or known Him [recognized, perceived, or understood Him, or has had an experiential acquaintance with Him"** (1 John 3:6 AMP).

Some people have wondered about this scripture and have said, "Well, everyone sins sometime. No one is without sin." This is not implying you will never sin. It means you will not deliberately and habitually sin. Someone who has a slack attitude that it's okay to sin as long as you confess it and ask forgiveness after you've done it, is deceived. It's not okay to sin. Sin destroys, but God provides a way to overcome it.

It is a fact that no one is without the possibility of sin. However, true Christians who are abiding in the Vine don't want to sin. They realize it hurts the One they love—Jesus. They also know that if they do sin, there is forgiveness and cleansing if they *repent*. First John 1:9 does say that if we confess our sin, He is faithful and just to forgive us of sin and cleanse us from all unrighteousness. However, there must be repentance.

Repentance is not just confessing sin to God. It is turning from the sin and walking away from it. It is hating the sin. This is the fear of the Lord (Proverbs 8:13). We are not afraid of God, but we are aware of sin's judgment and payment. Yes, there's always mercy with the Lord, but the attitude of your heart must sincerely be repentant.

This scripture is referring to those who do not have the fear of the Lord and continue in sin, wanting it more than their relationship with Jesus. Whatever you want or desire most, you'll do anything to get.

Purpose in your heart to let Jesus and His Word be your desire (Colossians 3:1). As you face difficult situations, continue in God's Word, for some of the richest, most abundant fruit has come from God's people at such times. **"Let the word [spoken by] Christ (the Messiah) have its home [in your hearts and minds] and dwell in you in [all its] richness, as you teach and admonish and train one another in all insight and intelligence and wisdom. . . ."** (Colossians 3:16 AMP).

The Father will be glorified as you bear much fruit. This implies that He only receives a little glory when we bear small portions of fruit or irregular harvests of fruit. People will see Christ through the stability and abundance of fruit in your life, and your heavenly Father will be glorified.

Fruit orchards which have produced abundant crops over the years are the ones which have been well cultivated, cared for and fertilized. Let the Word of God cultivate and fertilize your life. Keep watch over what has been planted in you so that you do not lose it.

Years ago at the end of our family's summer vacations, we would stop to pick peaches at a peach orchard in Arkansas. We would load our vehicle with peaches. After arriving home, my mom would freeze them for use in the months ahead. As I grew older, I remember the day we drove to the peach orchard and most of the orchard was dead. The people who owned it had stopped caring for it. There were acres of dead trees. They had not replenished the soil and protected the trees from insects. In a similar way, we must keep watch over our inner lives. If we don't take care of the tree and the branches of our lives, there'll be no fruit.

How is your relationship with Jesus? That's the whole foundation of your life. Is He still able to speak into your life, or are you simply trying to live your life on your own? Are you replenishing your heart and mind as you've given out? Have you continued to care for your inner man or have you neglected it?

Second Timothy 3:14-17 says:

But continue thou in the things which thou hast learned and hast been assured of, knowing of whom thou hast learned them;

And that from a child thou hast known the holy scriptures, which are able to make thee wise unto salvation through faith which is in Christ Jesus.

All scripture is given by inspiration of God, and is profitable for doctrine, for reproof, for correction, for instruction in righteousness:

That the man of God may be perfect [*artios* in the Greek meaning complete],[81] **thoroughly furnished** [*exartizo* in the Greek, meaning to prepare perfectly, to complete for spiritual service][82] **unto all good works.**

Webster says *continue* means to go on in a course of action; to last; to endure; to persist; to go on resisting any destructive influence or forces along the way.[83] Don't stop seeking God. We never arrive at knowing so much of God that we don't have to seek Him anymore in His Word and in prayer. Continue growing in Him. As we continue in Christ, we will have to resist destructive forces along the way.

Colossians 2:6-10 tells us how to continue in Christ:

As ye have therefore received Christ Jesus the Lord, so walk ye in him:

Rooted and built up in him, and stablished in the

faith, as ye have been taught, abounding therein with thanksgiving.

Beware lest any man spoil you through philosophy and vain deceit, after the tradition of men, after the rudiments of the world, and not after Christ.

For in him dwelleth all the fulness of the Godhead bodily.

And ye are complete in him, which is the head of all principality and power.

Verse 8 says, **"Beware lest any man *spoil* you. . . ."** In the Greek, *spoil* is *sulagogeo*, meaning to carry off as a booty or plunder; to rob and despoil. Why would Paul warn us if there was no possibility of being taken? This clearly shows the possibility of man robbing a Christian of his or her relationship with Jesus Christ and of God's blessings.[84] This doesn't contradict John 10:28-30:

And I give unto them eternal life; and they shall never perish, neither shall any man pluck them out of my hand.

My Father, which gave them me, is greater than all; and no man is able to pluck them out of my Father's hand.

I and my Father are one.

The word *pluck* in the Greek is *arpazo* and means to forcefully take them.[85] The way we leave out of His hand is if someone deceives us with wrong thinking or teaching and we choose to leave our position with Christ and take hold of deception or sin. God will always be there, ready to receive us back, but He will not violate our will to choose.

We must remain fully persuaded by continuing in the Word so we can recognize the deception of wrong teaching or influences that lure toward sin. We can't have inner strength to resist sin if we don't abide in the Word. We can't resist curiosity for more wisdom beyond the Word of God (like Eve) if we don't abide in the Word. God's Word is simple but profound and has all the answers to life. There is no wisdom of man that is greater. Time continues to prove this fact.

Ways To Become "Spoiled"

Notice the four ways a Christian can become spoiled according to the scripture from Colossians, chapter 2:

1. *Philosophy* - Webster defines *philosophy* as the love of or search for wisdom or knowledge; theory or logical analysis of the principles underlying conduct, thought, knowledge and the nature of the universe.[86] Throughout the ages men have searched for wisdom and knowledge of life apart from God. It's futile. How many universities and even some seminaries have presented man's philosophy as the highest truth, even above God's Word? How many young Christian men and women who had a genuine salvation experience have been *spoiled* while attending these universities and seminaries? Think about it! Some people have given up their spiritual upbringing and taken hold of humanistic lies because "Dr. so-and-so said you can't believe and base your life on the Bible." People need to be educated but not lose their spiritual life in the process. Thank God for Christian universities that educate and train the spirit, mind and body of students.

2. *Vain deceit* - Webster defines *vain deceit* as having or showing an excessively high regard for one's self, education, looks, possessions, ability, etc. indulging in or resulting in personal vanity; conceited; having no real value; empty; fruitless; unprofitable.[87] You can rise to the top of financial success; become the most beautiful or muscular as far as physical appearance; be at the top of the charts musically or an all-star in sports; get as many degrees in education as possible, etc., yet end up like the writer of Ecclesiastes. He did it all and found in the end all was vanity and vexation of spirit (Ecclesiastes 1:14). He concluded that the only thing truly fulfilling to man is to have the fear of the Lord and to keep His commandments (Ecclesiastes 12:13).

3. *Traditions of men* - Jesus said to the scribes and Pharisees that they had made the Word of God of none effect through their

traditions (Mark 7:13). *Tradition* is the handing down orally of stories, beliefs, customs, etc. from generation to generation; a long established custom or practice that has the effect of an unwritten law.[88] Traditions are not all bad, but they can rob the power of the Word of God if they are more protected, honored and revered than His Word and the freedom of flow of His Holy Spirit.

First Peter 1:18,19 AMP says:

> **You must know (recognize) that you were redeemed (ransomed) from the useless (fruitless) way of living inherited by tradition from [your] forefathers, not with corruptible things [such as] silver and gold,**
>
> **But [you were purchased] with the precious blood of Christ (the Messiah), like that of a [sacrificial] lamb without blemish or spot.**

Dake explains that at the time, the Jews had vain traditions and rituals. They had added innumerable religious burdens and empty ceremonies which they held to be essential to salvation.[89] Jesus came preaching and demonstrating the Gospel that blew away rituals and traditions and presented a personal relationship with God the Father through faith in Jesus' blood. Traditions do have the ability to spoil what God wants to do in a person.

4. *The rudiments of this world* - This is simply the world's principles and ways which are contrary to the Word of God. The world says, "Whatever feels good, do it." "There are no absolutes. You can't say something is absolutely right or wrong." "It's according to circumstances." "What you are in private doesn't affect what you are in public." "Vent your emotions."

As you can see, when someone lives by the rudiments of the world, they are going to have problems and they are going to cause problems for others. We could go on and on listing the world's way of thinking, but from these few quotes you can see that this way of thinking will *spoil* a person.

Colossians 2:3 says that all of the treasures of wisdom and knowledge are in Jesus Christ. As we continue to become rooted and built up in His Word, God will unfold to us His wisdom and knowledge that we need to daily walk out our lives, regardless of our occupation.

Second Peter 1:2-8 says:

Grace and peace be multiplied unto you through the knowledge of God, and of Jesus our Lord,

According as his divine power hath given unto us all things that pertain unto life and godliness, through the knowledge of him that hath called us to glory and virtue:

Whereby are given unto us exceeding great and precious promises: that by these ye might be partakers of the divine nature, having escaped the corruption that is in the world through lust.

And beside this, giving all diligence, add to your faith virtue; and to virtue knowledge;

And to knowledge temperance; and to temperance patience; and to patience godliness;

And to godliness brotherly kindness; and to brotherly kindness charity.

For if these things be in you, and abound, they make you that ye shall neither be barren nor unfruitful in the knowledge of our Lord Jesus Christ.

Peter tells us that by the promises of God (His Word) and through the knowledge of Him, we partake of His divine nature and escape the corruption that is in the world (and the lust for it). He says to be diligent, or make an earnest, energetic effort, to add these qualities to your simple faith:

- Virtue (or moral excellence; right action and thinking; goodness and morality).
- Knowledge.
- Self-control.
- Patience.
- Godliness.
- Brotherly kindness.
- Agape love (unconditional love; a love that is in spite

of what is done to you; a giving and forgiving love that is unselfish and does what will benefit others).

Then Peter concludes that if you are diligently seeking for these qualities to be in your life, you will never be unfruitful or barren.

Benefits of Abiding in the Vine

As we sum up the entire teaching of abiding and continuing in Christ and in His Word, let's look at the benefits of abiding in the Vine (Jesus Christ) according to John 15:

1. We will be called His disciples. **"Herein is my Father glorified, that ye bear much fruit; so shall ye be my disciples"** (John 15:8).

2. We will bring glory to God. **"Herein is my Father glorified, that ye bear much fruit; so shall ye be my disciples"** (John 15:8).

3. We shall ask what we will, and it shall be done. **"If ye abide in me, and my words abide in you, ye shall ask what ye will, and it shall be done unto you"** (John 15:7). To abide in God's Word is to delight yourself in His Word. **"Delight thyself also in the Lord; and he shall give thee the desires of thine heart"** (Psalm 37:4). The more we delight and abide in God's Word, the more His desires will be created within us. Then we will pray according to His will (according to His Word) and not to consume upon our own lusts. **"And this is the confidence that we have in him, that, if we ask any thing according to his will, he heareth us: And if we know that he hear us, whatsoever we ask, we know that we have the petitions that we desired of him"** (1 John 5:14,15). God delights in answering the prayers of those who are abiding in Him. Answered prayer brings Him glory.

4. Christ's joy will remain in us and be full. **"These things have I spoken unto you, that my joy might remain in you, and that your joy might be full"** (John 15:11). There is joy that stays with us no matter what happens around us when we are abiding in God's Word and His Word is abiding in us.

5. Jesus will no longer call us servants, but friends. **"Henceforth I call you not servants; for the servant knoweth**

not what his lord doeth: but I have called you friends; for all things I have heard of my Father I have made known unto you" (John 15:15). God likes to reveal His will to our hearts and commune with us as a friend.

6. He chooses to ordain us to go and bear fruit that remains. **"Ye have not chosen me, but I have chosen you, and ordained you, that ye should go and bring forth fruit, and that your fruit should remain: that whatsoever ye shall ask of the Father in my name, he may give it you"** (John 15:16). He chooses to use and promote those bearing His fruit because it glorifies Him.

7. We won't be cast away, but we'll be saved. **"If a man abide not in me, he is cast forth as a branch, and is withered; and men gather them, and cast them into the fire, and they are burned"** (John 15:6).

8. We'll walk in the God-kind of love. **"If ye keep my commandments, ye shall abide in my love; even as I have kept my Father's commandments, and abide in his love"** (John 15:10).

Abiding in the Vine will cause us to walk out the fruit of the Spirit in our lives. By abiding in Jesus, we bring glory to God and we bring His glory into the earth.

Endotes

[79] Webster, pp. 3, 138.
[80] Dake, p. 113.
[81] Vine, p. 846.
[82] Ibid., p. 468.
[83] Webster, p. 308.
[84] Dake, p. 231.
[85] Ibid., p. 107.
[86] Webster, p. 1069.
[87] Ibid., p. 1567.
[88] Ibid., p. 1507.
[89] Dake, p. 265.

CHAPTER 15
GIFTS BEARING FRUIT

I was raised in a wonderful Christian home. My father has been a United Methodist pastor for fifty years. Because of his exposure to the Pentecostal experience in his early years, he was open to the supernatural working of the Holy Spirit.

When my mother became hungry for the Holy Spirit, our family wanted to learn more and receive this dimension of God's Spirit. Since our denomination did not practice the gifts of the Holy Spirit as mentioned in 1 Corinthians, chapters 12 and 14, I did not know anything about them. I was taught on the fruit of the Holy Spirit, but did not understand the supernatural flow of the Holy Spirit in the believer's life.

As I became an adult, I desired to understand the gifts of the Holy Spirit. I realized that Scripture teaches us that God desires that we have both the fruit and the gifts of the Spirit operating in our lives for our benefit and for the benefit of blessing other people. First Corinthians, chapters 12-14, discuss the flow of the gifts and the fruit of the Holy Spirit in the believer's life.

In 1 Corinthians 12, Paul writes that we are not to be ignorant of the gifts. Then he expounds on the diversity of the gifts and their operations. Some people have explained away the gifts of the Spirit as natural, learned gifts rather than supernatural gifts. However, the gifts of the Spirit listed in 1 Corinthians 12:8-10 are not anything we acquire through natural education or training. They are given supernaturally to meet a need that cannot be met in a natural way.

Let me explain. We will divide the gifts into three categories. There are the revelation gifts, the power-working gifts, and the vocal gifts.

The Revelation Gifts

The *revelation gifts* are revealed by the Holy Spirit: the word of wisdom, the word of knowledge, and the discerning of spirits.

1. The gift of the *word of wisdom* is "the supernatural revelation or insight into the divine will and purpose, showing how to solve any problem that may arise."[90] It is the ability to foresee *future* circumstances so the person who is listening can make right decisions at the moment to avoid negative conditions later or to stand strong in the midst of circumstances. The gift of the word of wisdom can come to a person after prayer. It can also come through dreams or visions. It is divine insight that can come to a believer who is open and sensitive to hear the voice of God within.

For example, I knew a businessman who had been praying for his company, and in his prayer time he foresaw that if they took a certain direction, the company would be destroyed. When he told those in authority, he was laughed at and told that there was no way the company could fail. Because of leadership's encouragement, he left the job to go to work for another corporation. Six months passed and after ignoring the directions of this businessman, the company was destroyed.

In Acts, chapter 10, Peter had been praying at the noon hour and had a vision of a sheet descending from heaven which held many animals, some clean and some unclean. He then heard the voice of God say, **"Rise, Peter; kill, and eat"** (Acts 10:13). He said, **"Not so, Lord; for I have never eaten any thing that is common or unclean** [defiled or forbidden by the law]" (v. 14). And the voice of God said, **"What God hath cleansed, that call not thou common"** (v. 15).

Immediately following this vision, the Holy Spirit told him that three men were seeking him and that he was to go with them when they arrived. He went downstairs and met them at the door.

Before they could introduce themselves, Peter said, **"I am he whom ye seek: what is the cause wherefore ye are come?"** (v. 21). They told Peter about Cornelius, a Gentile, who had been informed by God through an angel to send for Peter to come to his house and hear the words he would speak to them. This was supernatural leading. By the gift of the word of wisdom, Peter knew ahead of time what was going to happen so that he would cooperate. Without supernatural intervention, he would not have gone with the Gentiles, but because of the Holy Spirit's revelation through the gift of the word of wisdom, Peter went. As a result, an entire household of people was saved and filled with the Holy Spirit. This was also the breakthrough of Jews reaching out to Gentiles with the Gospel so that all non-Jews could come to salvation through faith in Jesus. The Holy Spirit breaks down the racial barriers.

The purpose of the gift of the word of wisdom is to bless. I remember one time I had a knowing that I would sing and speak to a certain denominational ministers' gathering, but in the natural there was no open door for me to be received by this group. In an unusual situation, I was called to sing at the funeral of a district superintendent's wife, and all of the pastors from that denominational conference came to show their respect.

The night before the funeral, a lady from our own church in Tulsa, through the gift of the word of wisdom, said that I would prophesy at this funeral and that God would divinely open the way for it. Since this denomination did not practice the gifts of the Holy Spirit, I knew it would have to be a divine work of God. It happened just as she said.

There was such an awesome awareness of the presence of God in the service. God moved upon the husband, who was in charge of the service, to tell me to say whatever I felt to say before I sang. I respected him and shared in such a way that people didn't realize at first it was a prophecy. As they left the service, many of the ministers, with tears in their eyes, said they were inspired and had heard from God through my singing and prophecy.

Sometimes people feel they are on a mission to correct people everywhere they go, so they blurt out a prophecy with harshness toward people and there's no compassion in it. The result is that the people do not receive the person's word.

2. The gift of the *word of knowledge* is the supernatural revelation of divine knowledge or insight regarding past or present circumstances of a person to expose or reveal something.[91]

In Acts 5:1-11, Peter received a word of knowledge regarding Ananias and Sapphira lying about the money they had committed to give.

Several years ago, a minister we knew was going to invest a large sum of money, along with some other ministers, into a company that was going to help all of them in their productivity. The day this minister met with the man who was putting the deal together, his wife said to him in front of the man, "He's a fraud. We're not to do it." She had no way to know this, except by the Holy Spirit. Later, they found out that the salesman was a fraud and he had cheated several ministries out of thousands of dollars.

There have been times that as I have talked with people, God has shown me something about them to help me minister to them and speak a word of encouragement or warning into their lives. I remember one particular time when I had been leading worship and I felt very drawn to an individual. I prayed that God would open up an opportunity for me to speak to this person before she left the building. It happened.

As I spoke to her, I felt to ask if she was saved. The reply was "no." I asked, "Do you want to be?" The answer was "yes."

By the Spirit, I knew she was involved in a particular sin, but I didn't feel to confront it then. Sometimes the Holy Spirit leads me to confront a person. However, I believe there are times when the Holy Spirit reveals things to just pray for a person and let Him convict them. The fruit of the Spirit in this incident was to show this person that God loved them in spite of their sin, but He didn't want to leave them in their sin. Two weeks later, the person came to me and said, "I know you know. Please pray for me." I did and that day the person was set free.

3. The *discerning of spirits* is "the supernatural revelation or insight into the realm of spirits to detect them and their plans and to read the minds of men."[92] This gift enables the believer to see, hear, smell, or keenly sense angels or demonic spirits if they are actively involved in a situation.

In Acts 27:21-44, an angel of the Lord came to Paul and revealed what would happen to all the men and himself as the ship they were in struggled to stay afloat because of a hurricane. **"...be of good cheer: for there shall be no loss of any man's life among you, but of the ship"** (v. 22). The Lord had already revealed to Paul that he would go to Rome to preach the Gospel of Jesus, but then he also received the word of the Lord that all of the men in the ship would be saved from death on that trip if they obeyed and stayed in the ship.

In one of our last crusades in Russia, a Russian family shared with one of our staff workers about an angelic visitation that happened after an evening service. My husband had preached on the soon coming of Jesus Christ. When they returned home to their apartment, two men in white appeared to them. The entire family saw these two men and heard them say, "You can believe the messenger that you heard tonight. Jesus will return to earth very soon." Then the angels disappeared.

In Acts 16:16, Paul recognized and cast out the demons that were operating in the young girl who had been harassing him. In Acts 19:15, scripture reveals that the demonic spirits knew Paul because he had been casting them out of people.

I remember a young woman who came to our church one Sunday and was seated right behind me. Immediately I could detect the demons operating in her life. After the service, I turned to pray for her. Two other ladies were praying while I prayed and spoke into this young woman's life. She had come to pray against my husband and me during our service. She had not planned on being prayed for, but she could not see a way to avoid it.

After we had prayed for a while, the other two ladies and I began worshipping the Lord. She started to break and soon there was weeping and freedom. She shared how she had been involved in witchcraft and divination. She was set free that night. Since that time, she has kept in touch with us, and God is using her life to bless other people.

I've watched people at times who are so focused on casting out a devil that they forget that there is a person they are ministering to who needs not only deliverance from a devil, but compassion and divine insight to make them whole. True compassion is not weak nor is it afraid of any devil. Remember, Jesus was always moved with compassion to heal and deliver people.

The Power-Working Gifts

The *power-working gifts* include the gift of faith, the gifts of healing, and the gift of the working of miracles.

1. The *gift of faith* is "the supernatural ability to believe God without human doubt, unbelief, or reasoning."[93] *The gift of faith* is not the same as the simple gift of faith that is referred to in Ephesians 2:8 and Romans 12:3.

The salvation experience happens as a result of the simple gift of faith. Every believer in Jesus Christ has this gift. The supernatural gift of faith, however, goes beyond this. It is given for a moment or a season when the simple gift of faith is not enough. Sometimes circumstances are so beyond our natural ability to handle that we must have a miracle from God or it won't happen. This gift operates especially for *protection and provision.*

In Acts, chapter 28, when Paul and the men landed at the island of Malta, Paul gathered sticks for a fire and was bitten by a poisonous snake. God had told him that he would be brought before Caesar in Rome, so Paul simply shook the snake off into the fire and went on with what he was doing. The people who saw it expected him to die, but he was unaffected by it.

Paul knew he still had to go to Rome to preach Jesus Christ, so his destiny on earth was not yet finished. Because of the gift of faith that was in operation in Paul's life, all of these people accepted Jesus Christ that day.

This same gift of faith operates in people today who are standing for divine protection. I have friends in ministry who have been in circumstances where others have been harmed or murdered, but they have walked in peace. Some of the people around them have even seen their angels with them.

My husband has operated in the gift of faith at different times regarding ministry situations. It seems we've had numerous pressure times when we've had to pray for finances for land or buildings where, if the money had not come, we would not have been able to accomplish what we had heard from the Lord. However, the gift of faith would drop into my husband and he would know that it was going to happen. Each time has been supernatural, yet distinctly different.

The gift of faith drops inside a person after they have established God's will, and a peace that passes human reasoning prevails in the person until they see the fulfillment of what they believed. They don't worry, they don't vacillate, and they don't talk "what if." They do what they know to do and then stand.

2. The *gifts of healing* is "supernatural power to heal all manner of sickness without human aid or medicine."[94] The reason it is referred to as "gifts" of healing is because supernatural healing can flow in various ways—through the laying on of hands, calling out the gift of the word of knowledge, speaking the word of healing to a crowd or to an individual, acting out what another person has spoken to you to do, praise and worship, etc.

In 2 Kings, chapter 5, Naaman, the captain of the Syrian host, was struck with leprosy. His little servant girl suggested that he go to the prophet in Samaria to be healed. He went but the prophet sent a messenger out to meet him, instead of going to meet him, with a word to go dip in the Jordan River seven times and he would be healed. The captain was offended that the prophet didn't come out to meet him and that he asked him to dip in the dirty

Jordan River. However, because a servant urged him to do it, he did. Nothing happened the first six times, but on the seventh time, he came up out of the water, supernaturally healed.

In Acts 3:1-16, Peter and John were on their way to the temple and were approached by a lame man asking for alms. Instead of alms they said, **"In the name of Jesus Christ of Nazareth rise up and walk"** (v. 6). They didn't even touch him. The lame man acted on their word and, as a result, he was supernaturally healed.

Personally, I have experienced this flow of the Holy Spirit in praying for people and in singing healing songs. On one of our ministry trips to Albania, a twenty-seven-year-old man, who had never walked and had been crippled from birth, was listening to me sing "Rise Up and Be Healed in the Name of Jesus." He began to rock back and forth and then stood up and began walking awkwardly toward me. His mother began to cry and thank God, while others stood back and watched with amazement. As a result of his healing, all the people glorified God.

God wants to use all believers in healing. (See Mark 16:15-18.) Today many ministers pray for the sick and operate in the supernatural gifts of healing. Some ministers operate in calling out particular healings by the word of knowledge and people respond with confirmation of those healings. Others lay hands on people and they are healed. James 5:14 says to let the elders or leaders of the church pray and anoint the sick with oil and the Lord will raise the person up. God uses many methods to heal supernaturally through His people, and He uses yielded vessels to demonstrate His healing power to a hurting and sick world. Healing is God's demonstration of His love.

3. The gift of *the working of miracles* is the "supernatural power to intervene in the ordinary course of nature and to counteract natural laws if necessary."[95] Actually, any supernatural gift in operation is miraculous because it is beyond human ability.

In Acts 9:36, a woman disciple named Dorcas became ill and died. The people sent for Peter. When Peter came, he sent all of them out of the room and knelt to pray. Then he commanded life back into her body. She rose up from death, and Scripture says many believed and accepted Jesus Christ into their hearts that day.

Acts 8:6 says that people believed and gave heed to all that Philip the evangelist spoke, because they saw the miracles which he did—the healings of sicknesses and diseases, and people delivered who were oppressed or possessed by unclean, demonic spirits.

Many times, the gifts of healing and the working of miracles flow together. The Holy Spirit responds with whatever is needed. Several supernatural gifts can flow during the same time frame.

Years ago, a family who were neighbors to us loved us and believed in our prayers even though they didn't go to church. The mother always felt if they ever needed a miracle prayer, if they could just have Billy Joe or me pray, God would answer. They moved away to another state.

Years later, the oldest daughter showed up one Sunday at a Fourth of July service. She was unmarried and seven months pregnant. The doctor had told her, after x-rays, that her baby had a large mass attached to its head which was the same size as its head. The brain was inside of the mass, not inside the head. He suggested that she abort the baby. She told us that she knew if she could just get to my husband and me to pray for her, God would work a miracle and move the brain inside the head. She had told the doctor she would not abort the baby.

She repented of the sin of fornication and released her faith with us for a miracle when we prayed. Two months later, I was called to the hospital to go see her and the baby. She shared with me as her nurse stood by that when the baby was born, the mass was still attached to the head, but the brain had moved from the mass into the head. The doctors were able to remove the mass and stitch a small area in the back of the head where it had been attached. I saw the child and spoke with the nurse who happened to be a Spirit-filled Christian, and she confirmed what had happened. You could not even tell there had been a mass, except for the little line where the stitches were.

One year later, one of our staff members heard from the family. The baby was normal and experienced no further complications. Praise God for miracles! The love of God not only forgave sin but brought a creative miracle to a child who others wanted to get rid of because of the human impossibility of the situation.

The Vocal Gifts

The vocal gifts include prophecy, divers kinds of tongues, and the interpretation of tongues.

1. The *gift of prophecy* is "a supernatural utterance in the known language (or native tongue) of all those present. It is a miracle of divine utterance, not conceived by human thought or reasoning."[96]

In Acts 2:14-47, Peter, who had denied Jesus but had experienced the baptism of the Holy Spirit on the day of Pentecost, prophesied boldly what was taking place. He said, "This is the fulfillment of Joel's prophecy." That day 3,000 people were saved.

Again in Acts 4, Peter boldly prophesied the word of the Lord after the lame man was healed. As a result, 5,000 people were saved.

Prophecy exhorts, edifies and comforts (1 Corinthians 14:3). Prophecy can also contain the gifts of the word of knowledge, the word of wisdom and discernment. For example, Agabus the prophet came to Paul in Acts 21:11 and prophesied with a word of wisdom, **"Thus saith the Holy Ghost, So shall the Jews at Jerusalem bind the man that owneth this girdle, and shall deliver him into the hands of the Gentiles."** Paul knew this could happen, but he knew he had to go anyway because God had told him he would go to Jerusalem to proclaim Jesus Christ. Agabus saw into the future regarding Paul.

Anytime prophecy involves the revelation gifts, we must listen to our own spirit to judge how we will respond to the word given. We must also realize that as long as we are here on earth, **"We know in**

part, and we prophesy in part" (1 Corinthians 13:9). This means that sometimes the people who prophesy don't get the full picture, and God wants us individually to seek Him to know His direction.

There are also times when people simply like to hear themselves talk, and they are quick to prophesy to everyone they encounter. Many times these people prophesy out of their own mind or their own desires for others. This is why 1 John 4:1 says not to believe every spirit, but to test the spirits of the men and women who prophesy. Are they moving in compassion toward those they are prophesying to, or are they simply mad at everyone who doesn't look and think exactly like they do?

A prophecy can come through a few words spoken, a song, or a sermon message. It can be spoken in simple words, rather than in *King James* English! Prophecy is always in the known language of the people gathered. It is given to help people, not to destroy people. It will always be in line with the whole counsel of Scripture.

Even in the Old Testament, the prophets who forewarned of judgment and called people to repentance always spoke of God's mercy if the children of Israel would listen and do what God had spoken. The Old Testament prophets were willing to die for their people and the ones they had prophesied to because of their love for them.

2. The gift of *divers kinds of tongues* is "the supernatural utterance in other languages which are not known and have not been learned by the speaker."[97]

In Acts, chapter 10, God spoke to Peter in a vision to go with three men to the house of Cornelius. Once he arrived and began to preach and teach the people gathered there, the Holy Spirit fell on them, and while he spoke they all began to speak in other tongues and magnify God. Then Peter baptized them. Notice, they weren't even baptized in water yet. The Holy Spirit can do whatever He wants, however He wants, even if it doesn't fit into man's doctrinal mold.

They spoke in languages they had not learned. This also happened on the day of Pentecost (see Acts, chapter 2). Throughout the book of Acts, believers spoke in tongues when they were baptized in the Holy Spirit and they glorified God.

The gift of tongues is not limited to use in a gathering of people. It is for each believer to use daily. A friend of ours who was a nurse in a Tulsa hospital said that one day at work she had to give some medicine to a woman from the Middle East who could neither speak nor understand English. All of the doctors and nurses were frustrated with the patient because she would not allow them to give her the medicine.

My friend, Dorothy, prayed in her prayer language before going into the patient's room. When she went into the room, she felt she was to speak to the lady in tongues. As she did, the little lady's eyes lit up and she began to talk back to Dorothy in another language. Dorothy said she talked back to her in tongues, but didn't know a word she or the lady had spoken.

The lady allowed her to give her the medicine, and each day for the time that the lady was hospitalized, Dorothy would go into her room speaking in tongues and the lady would talk back to her with tears in her eyes. Dorothy said the doctors and other nurses observed her in amazement and asked, "Dorothy, when did you learn to speak in Spanish?" Dorothy replied, "I'm not speaking in Spanish or any other language I have learned. I am speaking in my prayer language." They said, "Well, whatever it is, it's working. Just keep doing it, because she's responding."

Dorothy later said, "I prayed and asked God that whatever we said to each other, somehow she would be saved as a result of it." I believe God answered Dorothy's prayer.

Paul said to the Corinthian church, **"I thank my God, I speak with tongues more than ye all"** (1 Corinthians 14:18). He taught them to pray and sing in tongues and in their understanding (1 Corinthians 14:15).

Jude 20 says that praying in the Holy Ghost builds us up in our most holy faith. In a gathering of people, however, when a prophetic gift of tongues is given as a message to the whole body, there must be an interpreter so others can understand what God is saying. Paul says in 1 Corinthians 14:26-32 that there is an order for a church service where only two or three should prophesy to the whole Body in tongues and interpretation. If there are several giving tongues and interpretation, it would take up the entire service.

3. The gift of *interpretation of tongues* is "simply the supernatural ability to interpret in the known language (or native tongue) what is uttered in the unknown tongue."[98] It is not based on an interpretation by a person educated in the particular language used, but by someone who does not know the language who interprets by the inspiration of the Holy Spirit. This is what makes it a supernatural gift.

First Corinthians 14:26 says that when believers come together, everyone should have within them something from God to give—a psalm, a doctrine, a tongue, a revelation, an interpretation—and each person should be willing to quietly listen to see whether or not they are to give out what they have.

If someone speaks in an unknown tongue, there needs to be an interpreter of the tongue. Everything is to be done in peaceful order, not in confusion. This requires the church leadership to direct the meeting as they sense God is leading. The other believers are then to submit to their direction in that setting.

As with all of the gifts of the Spirit, the motivation behind the operation of the gifts should be the fruit of the Spirit. Sometimes people simply want to be heard but do not necessarily have the interpretation of the tongue. Sometimes there is more than one person with the interpretation of a tongue so two people speak the word of the Lord that was given. Sometimes a tongue can be longer or shorter than the interpretation and vice versa.

I remember in one of our services when a tongue was given and someone else interpreted, neither of the people knew the language they had spoken or interpreted. A person visiting the service who knew the Hebrew language said that the people had spoken and interpreted in Hebrew. This has happened many times in churches where the gifts of the Spirit are allowed to flow.

Paul's Picture of Old Testament Types and Shadows

Now that we've defined the gifts of the Holy Spirit, let's examine the Scriptures Paul gave relating to Old Testament types and shadows in 1 Corinthians, chapters 12, 13 and 14.

In the book of Exodus, God told Moses to build a tabernacle in which He could dwell and to appoint priests who would minister to Him within the tabernacle. The priests were to wear long robes, with the hems lined with alternating pomegranate fruit and bells. The pomegranate fruit between the bells was to soften the noise of the bells. The bells were an Old Testament type and shadow of the gifts of the Spirit, while the pomegranate fruit was an Old Testament type and shadow of the fruit of the Spirit.

The bells were to sound when the priest walked from one area to the next so the people waiting outside would know that God was receiving the sacrifices for the atonement of their sins. It also enabled them to know that he was still alive, because there had been times when priests had not properly sanctified themselves and presumptuously went into the tabernacle (into God's presence) and died.

Notice, Paul explains the gifts of the Holy Spirit in 1 Corinthians, chapters 12 and 14, and devotes chapter 13 entirely to exhorting the Church to walk in the love of God. Originally, these chapters were written as a letter, with no division into chapters. However, when the Scriptures were placed in book form, the Holy Spirit directed the way it was divided because God does not do things by coincidence. Thus, in the division of chapters, Paul is teaching on the gifts of the Spirit, then on the fruit of the Spirit, and again on the gifts of the Spirit.

We need a balance of both the gifts and the fruit of the Spirit operating in our lives. Paul emphasized this balance as he explained how the gifts are to operate in believers' lives.

Paul said in 1 Corinthians 12:31, **"But covet earnestly the**

best gifts: and yet shew I unto you a more excellent way." Some people believe Paul was saying that love is the best gift and the more excellent way. However, the problem with this interpretation of Scripture is that love is not a gift, it is a fruit. Although love is the more excellent way, it is the way we are to move in the supernatural gifts.

First Corinthians 14:1 says, **"Follow** *the way of love* **and** *eagerly desire spiritual gifts,* **especially the gift of prophecy"** (NIV). Paul was not saying that the supernatural gifts of the Spirit should not be sought after. Notice, he says, **"Eagerly desire spiritual gifts."** The plural, gifts, causes us to realize that we are to desire all of the gifts in our lives. *The best gifts are those required for the situations at hand.*

For instance, if someone needs God's miracle intervention for provision or protection, they do not need the gifts of healing at that moment. They need the gift of faith and the gift of miracles. They might also need one of the revelation gifts, such as the word of knowledge or the word of wisdom, for direction.

Paul teaches the believer that every time someone operates in any gift, it should be out of the motivation of loving compassion for others.

Over the years I have observed that there have been times when some believers have operated in the supernatural gifts of the Spirit, yet have not moved with the compassion of Jesus. This is why some people have criticized the supernatural gifts of the Spirit. These same people have expressed that they would rather see Christians just walk in love and not even operate in the gifts of the Spirit. The problem with leaving off the gifts of the Spirit is that Jesus said, **"He that believeth on me, the works that I do shall he do also; and greater works than these shall he do; because I go unto my Father"** (John 14:12).

If we are going to be like Jesus and do the greater works, we will have to move in faith in the supernatural realm. The world around us is still full of hurting and sick people who need God's supernatural power in their lives if they are going to make it.

The majority of Jesus' ministry works was healing, casting out devils and operating in the revelation gifts of the word of knowledge, the word of wisdom and discernment. Some people have said, "Yes, but Jesus didn't speak in tongues." He didn't need to. However, He did command the disciples to go to Jerusalem to the upper room and wait to be endued with power from God and He would send the Holy Spirit on the day of Pentecost which had been prophesied by the prophet Joel in Joel 2:28. That day 120 people spoke with other tongues and prophesied.

The book of Acts has documented accounts of believers who spoke in tongues, prophesied, and moved in the supernatural realm of God, and it did not end with Acts, chapter 28. We, as believers, are the continuation of the church of acts here in this earth. (Note: Every New Testament author spoke in other tongues.)

Obviously, Scripture teaches us that we receive the Holy Spirit when we are saved, but there is a baptism of the Holy Spirit that endues [clothes] us with supernatural power from God.

In the book of Acts, each time believers received the baptism of the Holy Spirit, they spoke with tongues. This experience seemed to launch believers into operating in all of the other supernatural gifts. Still today, those who experience the baptism of the Holy Spirit are more prone to desire and operate in the other supernatural gifts of the Holy Spirit.

The supernatural gifts of the Holy Spirit are not a merit badge for any believer or minister. They do not make you any better than any other Christian. In fact, some Christians who have not experienced the baptism of the Holy Spirit have been stronger in attempting to walk in the character of Jesus than others who have just sought the power. The gifts of the Spirit are tools which equip the Christian to help and encourage others. This is why Paul wrote 1 Corinthians 13. He realized that some believers had wrong motives about the power of the Holy Spirit.

If a believer seeks to operate in the fruit of the Spirit—love, joy, peace, patience, gentleness, goodness, faithfulness, humility and self-control, then as he or she operates in the gifts, it will not cause confusion or bring hurt to people. The fruit of the Spirit will keep a person from using the gifts of the Spirit to control or manipulate other people's lives. The fruit of the Spirit will keep the believer in a submitted and accountable position with God and with church leadership. The fruit of the Spirit will direct the gifts of the Spirit to flow decently and orderly.

Believers who only seek the power of God and do not seek to grow in understanding the love and compassion of Jesus, will be offensive to others rather than helpful. Paul said in 1 Corinthians 13:1-3 NIV:

If I speak in the tongues of men and of angels, but have not love, I am only a resounding gong or a clanging cymbal. If I have the gift of prophecy and can fathom all mysteries and all knowledge [the gift of prophecy, the gift of the word of wisdom, and the gift of the word of knowledge]**, and if I have a faith** [the gift of faith] **that can move mountains, but have not love, I am nothing. If I give all I possess to the poor** [showing great benevolence and giving to the less fortunate] **and surrender my body to the flames [give your life or your body for a good cause], but have not love** [God's compassion, not just human goodness]**, I gain nothing.**

These are all wonderful things, but Paul emphasizes the motive of the heart *must* be God's compassion. He teaches us that whatever we do must never be done to make people think we are great. Our motive in operating in the Spirit of God is simply *love*. If this is our motive, it won't matter whether or not we become known by masses of people. Our fulfillment will be that we obeyed God and we moved in faith and love to help other people.

A checklist for flowing in the gifts of the Holy Spirit can be determined by the fruit of the Spirit that is being manifested. Check your motives:

• Do I truly love the people as I flow in the gifts of the Spirit?
• Do I operate in anger and harshness toward people?
• Do I want to flow in the gifts of the Spirit so everyone will recognize that I am somebody great?

• Are the gifts of the Spirit a merit badge that I wear to impress people?

• Do I want to flow in the gifts to have a name, such as "Prophet so-and-so?" (Some people who have focused on a name tag have fallen because of pride.)

• Do I feel I have to tell people that I am a prophet, or do I simply let God prove that gifting in my life?
Do I want to operate in the gifts of the Spirit in order to manipulate people?

• Am I willing to hold within me what I sense God is speaking in order to allow others to move out in the gift of the Spirit first?
• Or do I think that I need to speak every time I can so people will know that I operate in the gifts of the Spirit?

• Do I check myself to discern if what I sense within me is for me personally or for others? Is it simply for me to pray about, or is it for me to share?

• In a church setting, am I willing to wait and be recognized, or do I demand to be seen and heard?

• Will what I have to say bring encouragement and edification, or will it bring confusion or hopelessness?

In everything you do, let love be your motive and aim. **"...by love serve one another"** (Galatians 5:13). If we keep a servant heart as we flow in the spiritual gifts, we'll glorify Jesus rather than ourselves. With this attitude, Jesus said, **"...if any man serve me, him will my Father honour"** (John 12:26).

Endotes

90 Ibid., p. 175.
91 Ibid.
92 Ibid.
93 Ibid.
94 Ibid.
95 Ibid.
96 Ibid.
97 Ibid.
98 Ibid.

A FRUITFUL LIFE . . . WALKING IN THE SPIRIT

FRUIT	FRUIT ROBBERS	INSECTICIDE
Self-Control	Wrong Thoughts	2 Corinthians 10:4,5
Peace	Worry	Philippians 4:6
Joy	Discouragement	1 Samuel 30:6
Peace	Guilt	Romans 8:1
Peace	Confusion	2 Timothy 1:7
Peace	Fear	1 John 4:18
		2 Timothy 1:7
Love	Unforgiveness	Matthew 18:21,22
Love	Bitterness	Hebrews 12:15
Love	Envy	James 3:16
Peace	Strife	James 3:16
Love	Selfishness	1 Corinthians 13:5
		Philippians 2:4
Meekness	Pride	Proverbs 16:18
		Philippians 2:3
		James 4:6
Self-Control	Excessiveness	1 Corinthians 9:25
Faithfulness	Slothfulness	Hebrews 6:12
Self-Control	Critical Tongue, Gossiping	Ephesians 4:29
		1 Peter 3:10
Self-Control	Anger	James 1:19,20
Patience	Impatience	1 Corinthians 13:4
Gentleness	Harshness, Violence	2 Timothy 2:24
Self-Control	Immorality	1 Corinthians 6:18

CHAPTER 16
FRUIT ROBBERS

The diagram on page 193 reveals fruit robbers which try to destroy or damage the fruit of our lives as Christians. John 10:10 says the thief comes to steal, kill and destroy. The Word of God acts as a powerful insecticide which wards off pests that would try to rob the fruit from the vine or tree. Hebrews 4:12 says God's Word is **"quick and powerful"** against any fruit robbers.

Speak God's Word over your life when you sense the enemy bringing thoughts that are negative or contrary to what God has promised. You can also personalize the Scriptures as you speak them, such as, "I will not worry about anything."

Fruit	*Fruit Robbers*
PEACE	*Worry, care, or anxiety* – **"Don't worry about anything; instead, pray about everything; tell God your needs and don't forget to thank him for his answers"** (Philippians 4:6 TLB).
	Depression and sorrow - The Lord has appointed unto you that mourn or are depressed **"...beauty for ashes, the oil of joy for mourning, the garment of praise for the spirit of heaviness; that** [you] **might be called trees of righteousness, the planting of the Lord, that he might be glorified"** (Isaiah 61:3).
JOY	*Discouragement* - David encouraged himself in

the Lord. **"And David was greatly distressed; for the people spake of stoning him, because the soul of all the people was grieved, every man for his sons and for his daughters: but *David encouraged himself in the Lord his God*"** (1 Samuel 30:6).

PEACE   *Guilt or Condemnation* - **"There is therefore now no condemnation to them which are in Christ Jesus, who walk not after the flesh, but after the Spirit"** (Romans 8:1).

PEACE   *Confusion or Fear* - **"For God hath not given us the spirit of fear; but of power, and of love, and of a sound mind"** (2 Timothy 1:7). **"There is no fear in love; but perfect love casteth out fear: because fear hath torment. He that feareth is not made perfect in love"** (1 John 4:18). **"The Lord is my light and my salvation; whom shall I fear? the Lord is the strength of my life; of whom shall I be afraid?"** (Psalm 27:1).

LOVE   *Unforgiveness* - **"And when ye stand praying, forgive if ye have ought against any: that your Father also which is in heaven may forgive you your trespasses"** (Mark 11:25).

Anger and Strife - **"Let all bitterness, and wrath, and anger, and clamour, and evil speaking, be put away from you, with all malice"** (Ephesians 4:31).

"But if ye have bitter envying and strife in your hearts, glory not, and lie not against the truth. This wisdom descendeth not from above, but is earthly, sensual, devilish. For where envying and strife is, there is confusion and every evil work. But the wisdom that is from

above is first peaceable, gentle, and easy to be intreated, full of mercy and good fruits, without partiality, and without hypocrisy. And the fruit of righteousness is sown in peace of them that make peace" (James 3:14-18).

"Then came Peter to him [Jesus] and said, Lord, how oft shall my brother sin against me, and I forgive him? till seven times? Jesus saith unto him, I say not unto thee, Until seven times: but, until seventy times seven" (Matthew 18:21,22).

LOVE
Bitterness - "Looking diligently lest any man fail of the grace of God; lest any root of bitterness springing up trouble you, and thereby many be defiled" (Hebrews 12:15).

LOVE
Jealousy and Envy - "For where envying and strife is, there is confusion and every evil work" (James 3:16).

"Charity [love] suffereth long, and is kind; charity envieth not; charity vaunteth not itself, is not puffed up" (1 Corinthians 13:4).

PEACE
Strife - "For where envying and strife is, there is confusion and every evil work" (James 3:16).

LOVE
Self-centeredness and Selfishness - "Doth not behave itself unseemly, seeketh not her own, is not easily provoked, thinketh no evil" (1 Corinthians 13:5).

"Look not every man on his own things, but every man also on the things of others" (Philippians 2:4).

MEEKNESS *Pride* - **"Pride goeth before destruction, and an haughty spirit before a fall"** (Proverbs 16:18).

"Let nothing be done through strife or vainglory; but in lowliness of mind let each esteem other better than themselves" (Philippians 2:3).

". . .God resisteth the proud, but giveth grace unto the humble" (James 4:6).

SELF-CONTROL
Excessiveness - **"And every man that striveth for the mastery is temperate in all things. Now they do it to obtain a corruptible crown; but we an incorruptible"** (1 Corinthians 9:25).

"Let your moderation be known unto all men. The Lord is at hand" (Philippians 4:5).

FAITHFULNESS
Slothfulness - **"That ye be not slothful, but followers of them who through faith and patience inherit the promises"** (Hebrews 6:12).

LOVE, GOODNESS,
SELF-CONTROL
Abusive Words, Critical Tongue, Gossiping, Backbiting - **"Let no corrupt communication proceed out of your mouth, but that which is good to the use of edifying, that it may minister grace unto the hearers"** (Ephesians 4:29).

"For he that will love life, and see good days, let him refrain his tongue from evil, and his lips that they speak no guile" (1 Peter 3:10).

PATIENCE, GENTLENESS
> *Anger and Impatience* - **"Wherefore, my beloved brethren, let every man be swift to hear, slow to speak, slow to wrath: For the wrath of man worketh not the righteousness of God"** (James 1:19,20).

PATIENCE   *Impatience and Hastiness* - **"Cast not away therefore your confidence, which hath great recompence of reward. For ye have need of patience, that, after ye have done the will of God, ye might receive the promise"** (Hebrews 10:35,36).

> **"And the servant of the Lord must not strive; but be gentle unto all men, apt to teach, patient"** (2 Timothy 2:24).

SELF-CONTROL   *Immorality* - **"Flee fornication. Every sin that a man doeth is without the body; but he that committeth fornication sinneth against his own body"** (1 Corinthians 6:18).

> **"He that is slow to anger is better than the mighty; and he that ruleth his spirit than he that taketh a city"** (Proverbs 16:32).

HUMILITY   *Stubbornness and Rebellion* - **"Behold, to obey is better than sacrifice, and to hearken than the fat of rams. For rebellion is as the sin of witchcraft, and stubbornness is as iniquity and idolatry"** (1 Samuel 15:22,23).

ALL FRUITS   *Lack of Knowledge* - **"My people are destroyed for lack of knowledge..."** (Hosea 4:6).

CONCLUSION

How will the world see that Jesus is the answer to everything in their lives? How can we change the course of direction of this generation from destruction to life? Through you and me flowing in God's love, teaching and demonstrating the Gospel of the Kingdom of God.

In John 17:26 AMP Jesus said:

I have made Your Name known to them and revealed Your character and Your very Self, and I will continue to make [You] known, that the love which You have bestowed upon Me may be in them [felt in their hearts] and that I [Myself] may be in them.

Paul wrote in Ephesians 5:1,2:

Be ye therefore followers of God, as dear children;

And walk in love, as Christ also hath loved us, and hath given himself for us an offering and a sacrifice to God for a sweetsmelling savour.

If we choose to keep God's Word, His love will be perfected (or matured) in our lives (1 John 2:5). Your attention to God's Word is vital for you to walk in the fruit of the Spirit. It is hard to resist the lust of the flesh if you have not filled your spirit with strength to resist (Psalm 119:11).

Second Peter 1:3-8 tells us that God has given us great and precious promises to partake of His divine nature and escape the corruption (moral decay) that is in the world because of lust. Then Peter tells us how to walk in God's divine nature and escape lust: Give diligence (employ every effort) to exercise your faith, develop virtue (moral excellence), and knowledge along with self-control, patience, steadfastness, godliness, brotherly kindness and agape (God's unconditional) love. If these things be in you and abound, you will not become barren or unfruitful.

Books by Sharon Daugherty

What Guys see that Girls Don't...or do They?

Called By His Side

Avoiding Deception

Available from your local bookstore, or through Victory
Christian Center's Bookstore
918.491.7700

About the Author

Sharon Daugherty and her husband, Billy Joe, are founders and pastors of Victory Christian Center, Tulsa, Oklahoma (with a congregation of more than 10,000 people).

Raised a Methodist minister's daughter, Sharon made a commitment to Christ and accepted the call of God as a teenager. Music plays an important role in her life. She ministers in singing and songwriting. She oversees the praise and worship ministry at Victory Christian Center, and has recorded numerous cassettes and CDs.

Sharon is the Worship Pastor of Victory Christian Center. She teaches in Victory Bible Institute and ministers alongside her husband pastorally. Other ministry outreaches of Victory Christian Center include international radio, television, book and tape ministries and overseas evangelistic outreaches where they have established numerous churches and Bible schools.

Sharon has authored three other books: *What Guys See that Girls Don't...or do They?*, *Called by His Side*, and *Avoiding Deception*. Her music tapes include: Now Is the Time, Turn It Around, Stand Your Ground, Healing Songs & Scriptures, We Can Build a Dream with Love, My Folks' Favorites, Somewhere It's Snowing, Covered By His Love (protection songs and Scripture), Exalt the Lord, Prepare the Way of the Lord, and Catch His Fire (three live recordings of Victory Christian Center's praise and worship).

The Daughertys have four children and two sons-in-law who work alongside them in the ministry.

To contact Sharon, write:

Sharon Daugherty
Victory Christian Center
7700 South Lewis Avenue
Tulsa, OK 74136

*Please include your prayer requests
and comments when you write.*